1215/14
918/19

Put on Your Crown

Queen Latifah

Put on Your Crown

Life-Changing Moments on the Path to Queendom

with Samantha Marshall

GRAND CENTRAL
PUBLISHING

New York   Boston

Grand Central Publishing
Hachette Book Group
237 Park Avenue
New York, NY 10017

www.HachetteBookGroup.com

Printed in the United States of America

First Edition: May 2010
10 9 8 7 6 5 4 3 2 1

Grand Central Publishing is a division of Hachette Book Group, Inc.
The Grand Central Publishing name and logo is a trademark of Hachette Book Group, Inc.

Library of Congress Cataloging-in-Publication Data

Latifah, Queen.
    Put on your crown : life-changing moments on the path to queendom / Queen Latifah. — 1 st ed.
        p. cm.
    ISBN 978-0-446-55589-0
    1. Latifah, Queen. 2. Rap musicians—United States—Biography.
3. Television actors and actresses—United States—Biography. 4. Motion picture actors and actresses—United States—Biography. I. Title.
    ML420.L246A3 2010
    650.1—dc22

                              2009052863

Book design and text composition by L&G McRee

ACKNOWLEDGMENTS

Thanks to all those who have been a blessing to me. Especially my mom and dad, and my partner Shakim. May these words be a blessing to someone else.

Thank you Karen Thomas, my editor, for your patience and dedication, and Carol Mann, my literary agent, for bringing all the pieces together. LaWanda "LB" Black, my amazing assistant, for staying on the case and making sure I met my deadlines, and, finally, Samantha Marshall, for helping me bring my words to life in this book.

CONTENTS

Put on Your Crown

INTRODUCTION

I'll be honest with you. Before I started writing this book, I didn't have a clue about what direction to take. I knew I wanted to say something to girls and women that would help them build their self-confidence and bring out their inner queens. There seems to be an epidemic of lousy self-esteem in this country, especially among young women, and it concerns me deeply. We ladies have stopped putting ourselves first, and I wanted to share something with you that would help you feel empowered and make you recognize the individual and innate beauty that is you.

But whatever I said in this book, I wanted it to be authentic. I wanted to give you a piece of me from my heart, not some formulaic celebrity advice manual. You deserve better. Besides, I'm no psychologist or self-help guru. I never set out to be anyone's role model. That's too much responsibility for any flawed human being to carry. I can't tell you what to do. Who am I to lay down a bunch of rules? Where would I even start?

Then, just as my deadline was looming and my publisher was dogging me for a first draft, I attended a luncheon for female executives in the beauty industry. I found myself in a room full of confident and beautiful women. Seated near me were senior executives from Christian Dior, Estée Lauder, and Space NK. They were there to honor Esi Eggleston Bracey, the new vice president of global cosmetics for CoverGirl. This woman is impressive. She has a degree in engineering from Dartmouth College. She was Procter & Gamble's first African-American general manager. And at thirty-eight, she's also a glamazon with a standout look that's all her own. Her makeup was flawless, and she wore her hair cropped short, curly, and platinum blond, like a crown. As she got up to give her acceptance speech, I was curious to hear what this accomplished beauty queen had to say.

Her speech was peppered with interesting quotes, stories, and metaphors. But one thing stood out to me. Esi explained how her life was just a series of moments. We live from one moment to the next like heartbeats, she said, but every now and then there are moments that stop you, where you know everything is going to change.

That was it. Moments! I've packed a lot of living into my forty years, and that's exactly what I have to share with you—those moments when everything, present and future, changed for me. All those experiences that taught me something about how to live, love, and feel like a real queen.

Moments are all we really have in life, but they come and go so fast that most of the time we aren't even aware of what's happening to us. We're so busy worrying about the past or scheming to make our next move that half the time our moments—our lives—pass us by. We're too distracted to allow ourselves just to be and appreciate all the little joys that come our way.

I am truly a "live by the moment" kind of girl. The Sinatra song I recorded on my album *Trav'lin' Light*, "I'm Gonna Live Till I Die," is my anthem. I always try to take a big bite out of life and savor every flavor. "Before my number's up I'm gonna fill my cup . . ."

We can't get these moments back once they're gone, but we can choose to live them full out. We need to pay more attention to the present and what it has to teach us, because every so often you're going to have a moment that hits you so hard, it is truly life-stopping. I don't mean just life-changing. I mean life as you've always known it stops. You pause for a minute, taking in that feeling or truth the moment brings. It's like the wind gets knocked out of you for a second and there's this sudden feeling of recognition. Maybe your heart skips a beat, or your spine straightens, or the hairs on the back of your neck stand up. Or maybe you just feel more awake somehow. But from that point on everything changes, either by just a few degrees or by a full 180.

That moment, whether it's something wonderful, like the sudden realization that you're in love with somebody, or something terrible, like the news that you've just gone broke, will shape the rest of your life. Every following moment you live and action you take will be a by-product of the insights you gained and the hurt or the joy you felt. And you'll have a choice to make in how you respond: It can tear you down, or you can choose to see and hear what that moment has to tell you, learn from it, and decide where you go from there.

When that life-stopping event happens, it can bring real clarity to a situation. It's like the queen inside us is speaking the truth, and we'd be wise to listen. Good or bad, that moment is a gift, because it's a chance for our inner voice to cut through all the noise and tell us what we really need to hear. We can choose to ignore it and go on being victims, letting life's circumstances play us and push us this way and that. Or we can put on our crowns and fill our cups with the best that life has to offer.

More and more, women—from young girls to grown-up thirty- and forty-somethings—have gone deaf to what their best instincts are trying to tell them. We're sleepwalking on some path we think we're supposed to take. We're feeling the pressure to be a certain way and not be our true, authentic selves. Too many of us don't feel we're good enough. We worry if we don't have boyfriends or if we're not married with kids by a certain age. We stress if we haven't achieved some milestone in our careers or if we haven't bought a house and mortgaged ourselves up to the hilt like the rest of our friends. We beat ourselves up when we eat too many biscuits and gain five pounds. We put ourselves down and fuss and fret that we don't look like Halle Berry. Some women, who were beautiful to start with, even put themselves through all kinds of cosmetic procedures to look like their favorite celebrities or supermodels, and the results can be downright frightening.

What's with all this self-loathing? I read something the other day that made my heart sick. Females ages sixteen to twenty-four are more vulnerable to partner violence than any other group, almost three times the national average, according to a U.S.

Department of Justice survey. Teenage pregnancies are at an all-time high. HIV infection rates have soared, and AIDS is now the leading cause of death among African-American women ages twenty-five to thirty-four, according to the Centers for Disease Control and Prevention. That tells me young women in this country are facing a serious crisis in self-confidence. I believe the government is partly to blame for taking proper sex education out of the classroom, but there's more to it than that. Abuse and risky sexual behavior happen when you don't love yourself enough to say no or walk away.

Our younger sisters have it worst of all. The economy hasn't been this bad in living memory. You're leaving college deep in debt and with seemingly slim prospects of finding any job, let alone the career you'd hoped for. The unemployment rate for graduates is sitting at 46 percent and climbing. Man, that's rough!

Even though much of this is beyond your control, you probably blame yourself for not getting ahead like you thought you should. You're scared, and you feel like less than you are. Maybe your fear is making you hurt yourself by acting out. Maybe uncertainty about the future is paralyzing you and keeping you locked in an unhealthy situation. As I travel around the country, visiting schools and talking to kids, I see it all the time. My mother taught art at an urban high school in New Jersey for twenty-five years, and Ms. O, as she's known round the way, is still very much involved in the lives of her former students. She's shared some horror stories with me about what some of these girls are living through and doing to themselves. (Ladies, if this describes you, Ms. O and I want to reach through these pages and shake you by the collar. Then give you a hug.)

Hey, I've been there. I've lived the full range of low moments from the self-inflicted and stupid to the unspeakably tragic. One in four young girls has been sexually molested or abused in this country, and I was one of those statistics. As a teenager growing up in a working-class neighborhood in Newark, I also made some moves I'm not proud of. Money was tight, and I experimented with stuff that could have taken me right down into the gutter if I'd continued with it. To get to the point of true contentment with who I am, I guess I had to go through a few years of being something other than myself. Living in those dark places taught me to appreciate the light. I learned who I was and grew from these situations, and that gave me the confidence to reject a lifestyle that could have killed me.

I was blessed to have people around me, like my mother and father, who influenced me and kept me strong enough to pull myself right back up. They taught me how to listen to my inner queen and to

God. Moments of unconditional love from family and friends sustained me through the worst periods of my life, even the death of someone I loved deeply. That moment took me so far into the darkness that people were worried I'd never come back. I threw myself into activity so I wouldn't have to think. But every now and then, my brother's spirit would break through the noise and speak to me. He wasn't about to allow me to give up on life, and neither was the rest of my family.

I couldn't continue down that dark path because there were too many wonderful moments to come. Curiosity about life kept pushing me forward. From the time I was a child, my mother always said, "You can do anything." That simple statement stayed with me in good times and bad. I took those words to heart throughout my career. It never mattered what the haters said. I stayed true to who I was and refused to succumb to the stereotypes in the entertainment business.

My greatest happiness has come from giving myself permission to do me, on my own terms, whether it's singing on an album, acting in a movie role, hustling for a business deal, or just living my life and soaking up those moments of pure joy that come my way every day. I decided early on that I was going to put on my crown and rule my world by acting right and treating myself like a queen.

Not everyone is so lucky. Not everyone is surrounded by a nurturing family and positive influences. Maybe your teachers failed you and your parents are struggling too much with their own issues to tell you what you need to hear. Maybe all you've got is yourself. So listen up, in case you missed what your own life-stopping moments are trying to tell you. I'm writing this book to tell you that you *can* do anything! It isn't easy, but it sure is possible. I'm living proof.

Like I said, I'm not dispensing any hard and fast rules here. There is no single prescription for happiness or success. Everybody's different. You have to follow your own life's path and do what works best for you. Stop looking too much on the outside for affirmation. The trick is to discover who you are and what your passion is early on, then believe in yourself enough to go for it without compromise. Answer to yourself and your God, not to what others expect of you. Be yourself, have faith, and love who you are.

I've been privileged enough to meet some amazing people and live out some incredible experiences that have opened my mind to possibilities I would never have imagined otherwise. It's helped me live my life unafraid. I pursue my passions by jumping in headfirst. Sometimes I fail. Occasionally I get distracted. But I never regret trying because I have too much fun on the journey. I have no idea what's next for me, but I take joy in the fact that there are no limits.

I'm going to keep it real with you. Yeah, I've got wealth, and that eases the way on many levels, but don't let that be your excuse to dismiss what you read on these next pages. I take pride in being Every-woman. I have down-home values. When I'm at her house, my mom makes me take out the garbage just like everybody else in the family. I surround myself with the people I grew up with—*real people*—and they keep me grounded. Unless I've got something I have to promote for my business, I don't need to be at every A-list party. I relate more to you than most people I meet in Hollywood. Fame doesn't impress me. It's the regular girls and boys who make up my crew.

On these next pages, I'm going to share with you some of the life-stopping moments that shaped who I am today. Think of this book as an intimate conversation with Latifah, your older sister and friend. I've been out in the world, and now I'm coming back to sit with you and tell you about my experiences and let you know what I learned from them. Sometimes it's me talking, and sometimes it's other, wiser people speaking through me. I'll spill all that I can on these pages. I just have one request: Don't take my stories as blueprints. Instead, treat them as guideposts on your individual path to queendom.

The rest is up to you. Learning to love yourself is one of the hardest and most important things you'll ever accomplish in your lifetime. Self-esteem is a real skill that we've got to master if *we* want to blossom into our full, beautiful potential. Whether you are black, white, young, old, glitzy, plain, skinny, thick, shy, or some wild thing, you need to put on your own crown because you, like me, are nothing less than royalty.

Inside every woman there's a queen, and you owe it to her and to God to do everything in your power to live your most fulfilled and happy life. Don't let the moments pass you by. Let your inner queen's voice come through loud and clear. Be strong, be authentic, be you, and you'll do her proud.

Love,

Latifah

CHAPTER 1

Success

You are braver than you believe, stronger than you seem, and smarter than you think.
—WINNIE-THE-POOH

Looking up at that first mountain summit, more than four thousand feet in the air, I wasn't sure I could make it. It was at least fifteen miles, and the climb was steep. I'd never done a hike like that before. But there I was, with no choice but to put one foot in front of the other, making sure I didn't lose the fire trail and go wandering off in the wrong direction, or worse, fall down the side of a cliff. It was seven a.m., I'd been up since five a.m. for a yoga class and a vegan breakfast, and my first thought when I started that trail was, "We're going over *that*?!"

This all started early in September 2001, when I booked myself into a hiking boot camp in Calabasas, California, because I wanted to quit smoking. I picked up the habit when I was fourteen and managed to quit a few times, but smoking has a tendency to creep back into my life, especially when I'm working or stressing. A week in a healthy environment, doing nothing but hiking and yoga, was my way of separating myself from cigarettes and going cold turkey. This retreat was just a house in the middle of the woods. There were no stores around. There were no phones, except for a pay phone on the wall in case of an emergency. We all slept under the same roof and shared meals at a communal table. It was a place where people came to get back to some healthy living, lose weight, get in touch with nature, whatever it was. I just needed to be in an environment that was free of distractions, where I could focus on something besides my crazy, hectic lifestyle.

We were expected to hike at least fifteen miles of mountain ranges a day for a week, and that first time out was intense. I was out of shape and breathing hard. But as I continued to walk, I noticed something. I was feeling lighter. My mind was clear of all thought except for the present moment. I didn't have time to think about all the problems in my life. Or anything else. I was just concentrating on my feet, trying not to trip on a tree root while observing the view, breathing in the cedar-scented air, and enjoying the sights and sounds of the woods. I was back to the primal, the essence of surviving and getting to where I was going.

Eventually, I made it to the top, and when I looked down at the valley below me and the deep blue of the Pacific Ocean in the distance, I couldn't believe how far I'd come. I felt so strong and powerful. I was so proud of what I'd accomplished. I did it!

That night at dinner, the leaders of the hiking group went around the table and asked each of us to share a thought we had from the day. Everyone had a little story to tell or an observation to make. But when they got around to me, the only thing I could think of to say was this:

"I am stronger than I thought I was."

I didn't know I had it in me. There's more to all of us than we realize. Life is so much bigger, grander, higher, and wider than we allow ourselves to think. We're capable of so much more than we allow ourselves to believe. Box some seemingly mousy person into a corner and things will come out of her that you never would have imagined. If you push someone out of her comfort zone, she might perform in a way that she never thought possible.

We've all got so much more potential in us than we are willing to explore. We're all capable of second, third, and fourth acts. We're multidimensional beings, but we have a tendency to get trapped in a mind-set. We all deserve to get to that mountaintop and several more besides. We should be climbing the whole mountain range and enjoying the walk through all its peaks and valleys. And we can, as long as we remember to get out of our own way.

At the end of another one of those hikes, the other boot camp guests and I ended up on the beach in Malibu. We were so happy to be by the sea after several days in the woods, shut off in our own little enclosed world. I starting picking up rocks and throwing them in the water. Then I saw this one stone and did a double take. On it was an image of a man standing tall with one arm down by his waist and the other arm raised in the air with his hand clenched in a fist. It was a fist pump rock! I am not making this up. I believe in miracles, but trust me, I am not one of these people who see images of the Virgin Mary on a piece of toast! This was real. I showed it to the other people in the group, and they agreed—it was clearly a picture of a guy going, "Yeah, I did it!" It was like the universe was sending me confirmation of the message I'd gotten out of that week, and I was in a mental state where I was able to receive that message. In that moment, my mind was free of life's clutter and my eyes and ears were open to the signs. And guess what? Not only did I lose weight and improve my outlook, I quit smoking. Of course, it all got undone when I got back to New York City two days before September 11. From my apartment across the river in New Jersey I witnessed the attacks, and suddenly my world and everyone else's had changed. Recidivism bit me on the butt, and I went back to my bad habits for comfort. I forgot my inner strength.

Whenever that happens, I pick up that fist pump rock and contemplate its message. It sits on the mantelpiece of my house in Los Angeles, and every time I look at it, I remember what it's like to feel like Superwoman.

We all need a little keepsake like that, especially these days. I know many of you are losing jobs or struggling to find work. It's tough for someone who has just faced a layoff. Millions of us are feeling lost right now. This is a scary time for a lot of people. Their industries are dying. Men and women who worked in factories or at newspapers thought they'd have jobs forever. What they thought they'd be doing until they retire may no longer be an option. There's no such thing as job security anymore. The film and music business are no different. People don't realize that even if you make a lot of money, you can lose it just as fast. Show business isn't exactly a steady profession. One day you're hot, and the next day you're over. You never know.

One Door Opens . . .

But that doesn't mean it's over. Remember: *You are stronger than you think.* You have to go past what you think you can do, and then you have to go in and dig up some things inside you. Shake some stuff around. Take a personality quiz online. Tap into who you are as a person and then look around you. Go outside your comfort zone to figure out what you want to try, and when you hit on something that you like, you'll know it. When you're not watching the clock and you're completely absorbed in it, you'll know that's something you can dedicate yourself to 100 percent. That's the difference between a job and a career.

We all have talents and passions that can lead us into a vocation of some kind. A good friend of mine once told me that she didn't have any talent. I said, "Girl, what are you talking about? Everyone has a talent of some kind. Talent isn't just being an artist. It can be anything. You're just not seeing it yet."

As a matter of fact, I saw what *her* talent was before she did. When she finished college she got a job managing a Foot Locker store, and she was considered to be one of the best managers in the chain. I knew she was organized and reliable. She had a talent for follow-through. It was the perfect solution. I couldn't bring my business partner, Shakim Compere, on tour because our business was growing and he needed to stay behind at the office and run all our projects, so I asked her to come on the road with me as my business manager. It took a little convincing. It takes courage to leave behind a steady paycheck and benefits to try out something new. But this girl took that leap, and she proved to be a huge asset. She got the job done, and in this crazy business that's a talent to be highly prized.

Mad Skills

When I was starting in the business, most people in our crew could rap or do something musical. But not Shakim. He can't sing a note, and if he tried, you would hear dogs howl. But for two years I watched him. He was the guy who'd leave a party early if he had to go to work the next day. Everyone else would phone in sick or come in late. But he always showed up at wherever he was supposed to be, on time. So when I started performing around the clubs, he was the guy I wanted to handle my business. It's not sexy to pick up your own money when you've finished performing at a club. I'd ask various people to do it for me. Even Professor Griff of Public Enemy collected for me one time. But Sha was the most consistent and dogged about getting me my envelope of cash, counting it to make sure it was all there, and delivering. He has the strength of character to step away from the partying crowd, say no and stick to it, and tell people "Screw you" when necessary. Because of that, he has everyone's respect. No one messes with him.

At the time I made this decision, I was only seventeen, and Sha was eighteen. I don't know how I had the wherewithal to know at that age, but making him my partner was the smartest move I ever made. If I have a creative idea, he'll find a way to make it happen and blow it up even bigger than I could have imagined. He's the entrepreneur and I'm the artist, but we cross in the middle. Sha can be creative, too. When one of us comes up with an idea, we'll have a brainstorming session. One of us will say, "Hey, what about this," or, "I bet we can do that," and by the time we've finished we end up with a big ol' layer cake. Sha is brilliant at what he does. He has strength, determination, and intelligence, and he knows how to make the most of both our talents. I always tell him that I'm the star out there, but he's the star in the office. And if he didn't have the courage to tap into his skills, I wouldn't have been able to tap into mine and be where I am today.

I don't care what it is. If you're good at something and you love it, you'll find a way to make money at it if you persevere. Whoever started Sprinkles Cupcakes was probably someone who loved making cupcakes. I saw a story on CNN about some girls in Denver who do crochet bombing. Their mothers or grandmothers taught them how to knit, and now they go around throwing these beautiful crochet pieces over lampposts and architectural landmarks and taking pictures of what they created. They even put giant leg warmers on a statue of two dancers outside Denver's performing arts center. It looked amazing. These girls have a book out, and they're actually making money off this crazy idea. So someone in that crowd, who maybe wasn't as good at crocheting as the rest of her crew, was more business minded and started thinking creatively about ways they could tell the world about this new phenomenon they'd started. They said, "Guess what, we can make a video and put it on YouTube! We can go on CNN." They had their very own Shakim!

It Takes a Team

Most people don't have so much talent that they can become a success all on their own. We all need people to help us and lift us up. And other people need our help. When you put that together, you can create something really powerful.

When you're trying to reinvent yourself, it's important to connect with people who can bring out your strengths or who have strengths where you have weaknesses. You don't have to do it alone. There are so many creative people out there who are not tapping into their true abilities, and they have people around them who are probably feeling just as lost and scared as they are. Maybe they're about to lose a job, and they're wondering what to do next. But if you get together and talk about it, you may be just one conversation away from a great idea. Do some research, go on the Internet, make some calls, put in some time, and have the courage to take it to another level.

And don't tell me you're too old to try something new. The best teacher is a great student, so you should never stop learning. I don't care how old you are. My mother just turned sixty, and she's taking piano lessons for the first time. When I was a kid, I wanted to be a doctor. I'm not squeamish—I'm fascinated by the human body and anything to do with medicine and the natural world. Anyone would assume that path is no longer open to me, but not so fast. One of my favorite reality shows is TLC's *Trauma: Life in the E.R.*, and a couple of years ago I saw an episode about a forty-year-old medical intern. Most of his peers were half his age. But he just loved medicine and always wanted to be a doctor, so midcareer he decided to go to medical school. He's probably the oldest intern in the country and much greener than doctors who are years younger than him, but he has a lifetime of experiences he brings to what he does now, and that gives a whole other level of depth to what he does that his twenty-five-year-old colleagues don't have. And he brings a passion to his work, because he appreciates this opportunity he's been given to practice medicine later in life. He'll be successful because he had the guts and determination to follow his dream and make it happen.

In these times, you just can't assume that one job or career will sustain you for the rest of your life. Like Oprah said, you have to jump off the ship before it sinks. Don't be the person who stands there and watches it until it's bubbling under the water.

Ladies, I know I don't need to tell you, there is no such thing as job security anymore. That's why you shouldn't let a job define you. That's just a part of who you are, not the whole package. That's also why you need to diversify. Just like your investment portfolio should have stocks, bonds, a 401(k), and a savings account, you need to mix it up so that if one thing drops, you still have other stuff to fall back on. We've known this in the music business for a long time. A rapper who just raps isn't going to have much of a career. From the time he starts rhyming, he's

thinking about ways to expand his brand with merchandising and endorsement deals—if he's smart.
Record sales alone won't sustain him for the rest of
his life, unless he happens to be Jay-Z, and even Jay
makes his money from a million other things besides
his music.

I never really planned to do all of the things I do.
But I'm one of these people who crave variety. Case
in point: I love Asian food and tapas. My friends laugh
at me when we go to a restaurant because I always
have to order a few appetizers and entrées to share. I
always want to taste a little of this and a little of that,
especially if it's something I've never tried before.
The first time I went to Germany, I sat myself down
at a local bar and tried nineteen different beers. Obviously I didn't drink the whole bottle, but I wanted to
sample everything, because I'd heard Germany was
the place for beer. I love experiencing all the foods,
music, fashion, art, and architecture of different cul-
tures. But half of the people who are with me will eat
only at McDonald's, because it's what they know and
they don't like venturing into unfamiliar territory.
What a waste.

I feel the same way about my career. That's why
I called my last album *Persona*, with multiple versions
of myself on the cover and a blend of different musical
styles in each song. It was my way of saying, "You

can't define me." And there are so many more things I want to try before I die.

Talkin' About Evolution

People ask me how I managed to reinvent myself so many times over the years. They see all the things I do, and they assume they are second, third, and fourth acts. But the fact is, all the things you see me doing— my rapping, singing, and acting, the talk show, my brand building—were things I always had in me. I just didn't have the opportunity to show them all at once.

Reinventing yourself isn't becoming a different person. It's bringing out all the things you have inside of you in another way. I knew I wanted to be more than just a hip-hop artist. I thought maybe I'd rap and have my own management business on the side. But you never know where life is going to take you. There are so many roads, and sometimes they lead you to places you'd never imagine. The thing about following your passion and living in the moment is that you're able to see more openings than most people and have the courage to jump through those doors.

Try Your Best

I was lucky. I grew up in a home where my parents were always encouraging me to try my best and just go for it. Didn't matter what it was or whether I was brilliant at it, as long as I gave it my all. That made me unafraid to fail. I had the courage to try different things purely out of a curiosity or a passion, and as long as I applied myself and gave it 100 percent, Mom and Dad were always proud. I might have come home cut from a team or upset that I'd stumbled at something, but they'd dry my tears and say, "Did you try your best?" And if I said, "Yeah, I did try my best," they'd say, "Well then, good for you! Be proud of yourself!" And I was.

My dad, Lancelot Owens, was determined that I would never cower in a corner. If I wanted to try something, he told me to just go out and do it, no excuses. When we were growing up, my father treated my brother, Winki, and me as equals. If Dad and Winki were playing football, I was playing football. If Winki was going to a dojo to take a martial arts course, I was gonna learn a few defensive moves, too. Why not? Because I was a girl? Didn't matter. Dad wanted to build up the competitor in me. He was a cop and a Vietnam veteran, and he wanted both of his kids to develop a certain strength of character.

He wanted me to have the confidence to be able to stand up for myself in the mean streets of Newark. He used to say to me, "Dana, just because you're a girl, don't ever let anybody tell you that you can't. I know you can!" For a black man of his generation, that was pretty progressive. My dad's always been about equal opportunity. And like equality, opportunity isn't limited to gender or race or anything else. You make your own opportunities.

The Perfect Partner

My parents gave me the foundation. But I was especially fortunate to have Shakim with me from the beginning. He always knew what I was capable of. We've been friends since I was fifteen and he was sixteen going on seventeen. He was a student in my mother's art class at Irvington High School. He's seen me sing, rap, act, joke around, and hold my own in conversations with people from all kinds of backgrounds. He's seen me be outgoing. He's seen me show up when it was time to show up. He knew me in a way the rest of the world had yet to witness at the beginning of my career. He knew that the acting bug bit me when I was in a school play, and he encouraged me to pursue it. He knew that I didn't want to be just an R&B singer and that I loved jazz. He knew before I did that I'd be just as capable of hosting my own talk show as I am at developing a new line of cosmetics or perfume or clothing. So what looked like reinventions were really just moments when I had the right time and opportunity to let all these things inside me out into the universe. A lot of the time, Sha's job is to make sure those doors are open to me. He's been amazing at providing me with a road to follow.

We all need someone in our lives who can see what we're capable of and bring it out in us. So don't shut anyone out. Everyone can be a friend, and anyone might be able to help. There's an old saying, "A wise person knows many things, but a successful person knows many people." We can't do it alone. Other people can change our lives and take us a lot further than we ever thought we could go. That's what Shakim did for me.

A lot of people in my business are surrounded by yes-men and -women. There's always someone around you to pump you up and tell you everything you do is great. They blow smoke up your behind and tell you, "Oh, you're so cool, you're so funny," you're so this, you're so that. You rarely hear the word "no." And what that does is create a false identity. When people are telling you "yes" all day, you never get a sense of who you are or where you really stand. But I have real people in my life who let me know. They pat me on my back when I do good and spank me when I do bad. That's Shakim. He always tells me the truth. He's my barometer.

I'm very involved in my career and pretty clear about where I stand, but Sha helps me stay close to what the truth is. He lets me know when I'm deficient in something, and he tells me what people think and what the temperature is on certain things. He helps me keep it all in perspective, so I never think I am bigger or smaller than I really am.

Start Where You Are

You need to start with that. It's important for us to figure out who we are as quickly as possible. We need to be clear on what we are and are not willing to stand for, deal with, or put up with. We need to decide who we want to be seen as. The quicker you figure out your insecurities, deal with them, and learn how to love yourself, warts and all, the better off you'll be. Because then you'll be making decisions and choices based upon your authentic self. You'll have the confidence to chase down your dreams instead of phoning in whatever it is you think you're supposed to be doing.

I have confidence to spare, but that doesn't mean I'm great at everything I do. I don't make a record expecting to go platinum. I make music because something inside me is aching to get out, not because I have to make the top ten on the *Billboard* charts (although a hit is always nice). My first records only went gold, but they were enough to launch a twenty-year career. One of the albums I did, *Order in the Court*, didn't turn out like I'd hoped. To be honest, it was pretty mediocre. The record label was going through a whole regime change, and the album didn't get the kind of support it could have. And musically, I was trying to do something a little different that didn't quite work. But I was okay with that, because I know I gave it everything I had, and the experience taught me things that made me better.

My talk show wasn't a raving success, either. If it was, I'd still be doing it. Things got really heavy with my guests and the studio audience. Every day I felt like a doctor going into the ER, and you lose patients sometimes. It's exhausting, because after that you have to go home, process what happened, dust yourself off, and come into work the next day ready to save lives again. Again, I tried my best. But you can't beat Oprah at her game.

Be on Time to the Spot, Get the Look, Nail the Shot

The movies I made weren't always huge box office or critical successes. Sure, I want them to earn millions at the box office on opening weekend, but it doesn't always work out that way. I show up on time, prepared and ready to go. I remember my lines, hit my marks, and deliver my performance to the best of my ability, with all the heart, authenticity, and emotion that the role requires. I work well with my co-workers, shoot the stills, go on the press junkets, and do everything I can to promote the movie in every possible way. I can't say what the studio does or what the director, producer, or some other actor does, but I sleep at night knowing I did my best. If a particular movie doesn't go so well, I can't say anything about the audience. Maybe ours was released in eight hundred theaters and another one was released on the same day in two thousand theaters. But two years later, if people find it on cable and decide it's their favorite movie from me, I'll know it's because I did my best. It's going to show.

It might not be when or how you want it to happen, but you don't have to feel bad about it. Try your best, then you can let that thing go and try something else. Just be sure to finish what you start. See it all the way through, and don't give up so easily. It's human nature to want immediate satisfaction, but sometimes these things work out best on God's schedule, not your own. And sometimes His plan is a lot more interesting than anything we can come up with ourselves. It's hard to see it at the time, but maybe losing a job is a blessing, because it frees you up to pursue something that you find more fulfilling. Maybe you wouldn't have done it if your back hadn't been against the wall.

Renaissance Woman

You don't have to love just one thing or have only one career. Don't be like my scared ass friends when we were on tour in Europe. Don't take the McDonald's approach to your life's work. Sure, the familiar is comforting, but it's also boring. You'll miss out on so much flavor in life. Order up a few tapas dishes. Taste something new on the menu!

You can love many things. Give them all the energy, time, love, faith, and strength that you have. Frederick Douglass said that without struggle, there can be no progress. No one ever got ahead by going through the motions. You have to be constantly improving your-self. Make your life the masterpiece you want it to be.

You are multifaceted. As human beings, we have so many sides to us. Use all of your ability and talent and the knowledge you gained along the way that you didn't even know you had. Do your homework and step out on the faith and conviction that you can do it, and while you're at it, send up a few prayers. Ask that your path be guided and directed, and it can happen if you can step out of your own way.

Learn what you are capable of, and evolve. Knowing who you are doesn't mean you have to put yourself in a box. A healthy identity has to be given room to breathe and grow.

I'm not done yet. I will be a work in progress until the day I die. There's a lot more to this party called life, and I am going to extract all I can until the party's over. I want to do something great every year and see it through to completion, whether it's expanding on my acting roles, producing more movies, learning more things, or doing something for others in a way that has a huge impact. I want to learn to fly a plane. I want to write more songs. And many other things besides.

I'm going to stay on this path of self-discovery, even when it's a steep uphill climb, just like that mountain that seemed so high, I never thought I'd make it to the top. But I did it, and I did it the way I do everything else—step by step, moment by moment. That's all you can do. Face each challenge as it comes. Don't look up and let yourself be defeated before you even start. Just focus on the journey, and before you know it, you'll get there. And when you finally do make it to the top, you'll feel so proud and so energized, you'll be ready to conquer that next mountain. You'll know that it was worth every stumble and scrape along the way. You'll also discover that, yes, you *are* stronger, swifter, and smarter than you think.

CHAPTER 2

Beauty

In diversity there is beauty and there is strength.
—MAYA ANGELOU

I was loving the camera, and the camera was loving me. Hot music was thumping on the sound system, scented candles filled the room with a delicious aroma, and the lighting was as clear as the early morning sun. The energy at that photo shoot was electric. People were dancing. But everyone on that set, from the ad executive in charge of the campaign to the assistant in charge of keeping my glass filled with water, was focused on one thing: making my first CoverGirl moment perfect.

And it was. Earlier that day, I'd spent more than three hours in hair and makeup. The clothes were beautiful. My hair was long, smooth, and glossy. My complexion looked flawless. The makeup artist knew every trick to bring out the brown and golden tones of my skin. He sculpted my cheekbones, perfected my pout, elongated every single one of my lashes, and made my eyes smolder with shadows and liner. I'd done photo shoots with hair and makeup people before, but never like this. The so-called glamour part of my life was always kind of rushed—something I had to squeeze into a jam-packed schedule. But for this picture, they were going to take their time and do it up right. All the attention and primping truly did make me feel like royalty.

But the best part of the day was seeing those first proofs for the ad. They were gorgeous. It was a whole new look for me—pretty, feminine, almost angelic. I wish every woman could have a moment like that. The photographer brought out all the beauty I thought I always had and then some. He shot me gazing away from the camera, an angle I tend to prefer. There's something sort of dreamy about those shots that say your mind's in a different place. You almost want to travel there. It was so gorgeous, and I felt really proud—of CoverGirl for understanding the fact that there are different types of beauty out there besides size zero blond models, and of the example it was going to set for girls who are not the typical ideal of beauty. They were going to look at this ad in some magazine. I could just hear them saying, "Wow, she's a cover girl; I can be a cover girl! She can sing and act and be a beautiful woman in a magazine, and I can be all those things!"

It wasn't so much that this moment was pivotal to my self-esteem. I always felt beautiful in my own way. My CoverGirl moment had an impact in the sense that it boosted my confidence by a few degrees. But I believed it would completely change the lives of millions of girls, and that gave me a thrill. I knew CoverGirl was going to spend a shitload of money on this campaign. This ad was going to be everywhere. It was going to expand the idea of beauty in a way that was long overdue. Young black, Latina, Indian, and Asian girls would see it. The image would be in their faces on a daily basis. Some kid would look at it, have her own life-stopping moment, and say, "Okay, beauty *is* me."

More Shapes, Colors, and Sizes, Please

When I was coming up, there were no women who looked like me in the media. As a kid, I'd flip through magazines like *Essence*, *Ebony*, and *Jet*, staples in any African-American household, and for the most part the models were light-skinned and skinny. My mom would sometimes bring home *Vogue* and *Harper's Bazaar*, where black models were practically nonexistent. I'd flip through these big, thick books, fascinated by all the wonderful products and gorgeous, cutting-edge fashion and accessories. But they were practically devoid of people who looked like me, or my mother, or my aunts—beautiful women in their own right. Maybe there were one or two models who looked like my friends' Spanish cousins, but that was about it. It kinda hurt that what was supposed to be the epitome of all that was desirable and edgy and fashionable had no relevance to me. Nothing was tailored to black women, especially not me and my curvy, darker-skinned sisters. It was as if Madison Avenue was telling us, "This isn't for you."

There are a few more black models today. There are even one or two curvier girls on the magazine covers. But diversity in the fashion industry is all too rare. You still hear stories about photo editors digitizing images beyond recognition. A little airbrushing in the industry is normal and acceptable to some extent. Sometimes you might have a pimple or the lighting has cast a shadow or a piece of clothing has fallen the wrong way. But when they start lightening up the skin of gorgeous black women like Beyoncé or Jordin Sparks, and when they start chopping off the curves and body parts of perfectly normal women to make them look gaunt and sickly, like they did in that Ralph Lauren ad, it's time to draw the line.

Every day, girls are being exposed to standards of beauty that aren't even real. They're just images manipulated by a photographer. I know, because I see these women—actresses, models, and singers—in the flesh, and they are much more beautiful in their flawed individuality than their cookie-cutter images in a magazine spread. Nor do they look like those distorted paparazzi shots the tabloids like to print. You can make anyone look bad when you shoot them at an unflattering angle. But to say beautiful, healthy women like Tyra Banks or Jennifer Love Hewitt are fat is just sick.

Hollywood is this unrealistic bubble that doesn't represent the rest of the country, but its influence has spread far and wide. You see all these actresses starving themselves to look amazing on the red carpet, and the young girls across America who try to emulate that starved physique end up slowly killing themselves. A lot of people in the entertainment business have eating disorders. They get pressured by their agents, producers, and studio executives to lose weight. At all these award dinners and luncheons I get to go to, you almost never see young actresses touch their food. Many have way too much plastic surgery. I don't knock the profession; it has its place. But people get addicted. So many women, and men, are chasing an ideal of beauty that's just not cute.

What is it that these ladies see in the mirror that would make them think it's a good idea to blow up their lips with some filler to the point where they look like two hotdogs on their face?

When you strive for that kind of perfection in your appearance, you end up not looking human. Women lose their individuality, and they look like sisters from the same planet. Girls are taking drugs, diuretics, and laxatives to get thinner and thinner. They're doing all sorts of things to themselves short of mutilation in their quest to look like Angelina Jolie, and the people behind the magazines and blogs are perpetuating this madness as they sit and judge every little hair that's out of place. It sets a terrible precedent for the rest of women and girls. When you give way to this kind of obsession with your looks, you miss out on what true beauty is.

Perfectly Imperfect

To me, real beauty has nothing to do with perfection. It's those little flaws we have in our faces that make us memorable. It's like a great jazz performance, when a horn or saxophone cracks a bit in one spot. Or one of those rare times Aretha Franklin hits a note that's ever so slightly off. Those are my favorite parts. It isn't perfect, and that's okay. It's all part of the charm. The way it is, flaws and all, is special, and that's better than perfect. Not only do these tiny imperfections highlight how brilliant the rest of the performance is, they remind me that the artist is human, and that makes their music even more beautiful to my ears.

Leave It Alone!

The most beautiful picture of Mary J. Blige I ever saw was the one on the cover of her album *Mary*. It's a black-and-white shot of her in profile, and it shows the scar she has running down from her left eye to the top of her cheekbone. Usually that little mark gets airbrushed out, but the fact that they left it alone is what makes this image so unforgettable.

For the most part, I've been fortunate that photographers have not gone crazy and digitized my image beyond recognition. But I have had issues with the scar on my forehead. Sometimes I have to fight to make sure they leave it alone. I got that scar when I was three years old playing tag with my brother. I tripped and fell, hitting my forehead on the corner of the bathroom door frame on the way down. Not long after that, I was running into my aunt's house when I tripped and landed face-first on the stairs, in the exact same spot where I'd injured myself before. I had to have three stitches. But that scar reminds me of my childhood and the fun times I had with my brother. It's part of who I am. I *love* that scar!

I wish every woman would learn to love herself and embrace what she was given naturally, even her small imperfections. The point is to be healthy, feel good in your own skin, and play up your best assets. Whether you're short or tall, thick or thin, the beauty comes from how you carry yourself, how you care for your appearance, and the inner glow that confidence brings. A girl can be born plain, but if she believes herself to be gorgeous, she can be the sexiest woman in the room.

When your self-confidence is low, it's all too easy to internalize what you see or don't see in the media. I was fortunate enough to have a foundation of self-love instilled by parents who constantly told me how beautiful and special I was. As a little girl, I never wondered whether I was beautiful or not. I knew I wasn't pretty in the conventional sense, and all the Dark and Lovely in the world wasn't going to get my hair straight, but I liked myself plenty.

I was athletic and big-boned. All limbs. I was always running around, getting scraped up, ripping up my dresses, and losing my hair clips, but inside I felt every inch a girl. When my cousin Sharonda showed me her father's book of Muslim names and I came across "Latifah," I decided that had to be my new name, because it meant "delicate, sensitive, and kind." That was exactly how I felt inside.

Who You Callin' a Tomboy?

But at every stage in life, people come along who test your self-esteem. There's always going to be someone who's going to try to tear you down. Self-love is something we have to work hard at every day. As filled as I was with love at home, outside in the world of schoolyards and Newark streets it was a different story. In fourth grade I changed schools, and I was very much the new kid trying to join in at recess. Instead of playing hopscotch or drawing on the concrete like the other girls, I was drawn to whatever sports the boys were playing, whether it was football, softball, or basketball. I'd always played these sports with my dad and my big brother, and I was good at all of them. But that didn't seem to matter to my new classmates. They'd all been together since kindergarten, and they were determined to let me know my place. There was a kid named Andrew, a typical alpha male, and he put himself in charge of all the sports teams. When it came time to pick the players, he'd always choose me last, if at all. Boys are under their own pressures from their peers. They don't want some girl showing them up and getting a basket or a hit on them, and I guess the fact that I was so competitive in sports made me a threat.

Pretty soon, the boys in school started calling me a tomboy, and they didn't mean it in a gentle, teasing kind of way. They were saying straight out that I somehow wanted to be a boy and that I wasn't pretty or cute the way a regular girl should be. I hated that word, and I couldn't fathom why they were saying it to me. It especially hurt when Wink called me that. (It soon stopped when he realized how much it upset me.) One day I felt so bad, I came home to my mother, crying, "Ma, why are they calling me a tomboy?"

My mother said, "Dana honey, you're not a tomboy. You're just athletically inclined."

Now, try telling that to a bunch of schoolkids on a blacktop in New Jersey. But the next time the taunts came, I did just that. I told Andrew, "I'm not a tomboy, I'm athletically inclined!" Of course, it didn't go over too well. But I said it with all the backbone I could muster. At first, he looked dumbfounded. Then he laughed, and the whole schoolyard joined in. But this was what I had to do. It was more an idea for me to have in my own mind. With all my nine-year-old wisdom, I decided I was not going to feed into what people said about who I was. I was not going to let other kids define me. I chose instead to define myself, even if it was in a completely ridiculous way. And guess what? Pretty soon after that, other kids started picking me first to play on their teams.

Self-esteem starts early in life. We begin with a clean slate, but it gets junked up fast. As children, we are so vulnerable to the stereotypes people want to heap on us. It seems like everyone has an idea of how we're supposed to be from the time we can crawl. This is especially true for girls. All too often, our self-esteem is tied up in our looks. Our bodies get scrutinized and criticized from the minute we start developing. And when we're a little thicker than the feminine ideal dictates, it's even worse. That's why we need to be strong and love ourselves for the fact that we are about so much more than our looks.

Love Yourself

Gabby Sidibe, the star of *Precious*, plays a character who's tortured by the people around her for the way she looks, but in real life she's bubbly and happy, nothing like the character she plays. I love what she has to say about this: "I sleep with myself every night and I wake up with myself every morning, and if I don't like myself, there's no reason to even live the life. I love the way I look. I'm fine with it. And if my body changes, I'll be fine with that."

The more people like her express that message, the more girls who come after us will believe it, and at an earlier age. This is wisdom that could change the world if we live it every day.

But even when we're blessed with Gabby's hard-won self-confidence, there will be moments when we fall prey to low self-esteem. Anyone who says she's confident 100 percent of the time is either fronting or delusional. It's okay to have some ups and downs. I do.

Those moments started in my early adolescence, when I began developing faster than most girls my age. I wasn't heavy so much as big-boned. I was athletic, and I had that ungainly walk that young girls have when they're all limbs. We're like certain big breeds of dogs when as puppies they start their first growth spurt and their minds haven't caught up to their bodies yet. I tended to hunch over. I didn't have that cutesy, girly walk that my other friends had naturally. Instead I felt awkward. I see a little of me in President Obama's oldest daughter, Malia. Both of her parents are tall and athletic, and so is she. And she has that same slightly lumbering, gangly gait I had. No doubt Malia is going to grow into someone as graceful as her mother soon enough.

Walk Tall

To get me through my awkward phase my mom started teaching me how to walk with a book on my head, like the models. It was our time together, when we got to be girls. I was running around with my father and brother so much, playing football, going fishing, and doing all the fun stuff that boys usually do, that I think this was Mom's way of balancing out their influence with some of her own. But these small moments we had together ended up having a huge impact on my self-esteem because they taught me how to walk tall. In her own subtle, gentle way, my mother was instilling in me the importance of holding myself upright and being a lady.

It was a simple thing, but mastering that strut was a blessing, especially by the time I hit high school. It gave me a presence when I walked down those halls. It was a big boost to my sense of self-confidence, power, and pride. I wasn't one of those introverted kids who walked with my head down, holding my books close. I walked around like I had an "S" on my chest. There is something about moving through the world with your head held high that says, "I am proud to be who I am." People react to you differently. They *see* you. You project this idea that you think you are pretty damn special, and the rest of the world gets convinced by your body language. This was not a walk that said, "I'm hiding myself because I'm not worthy." This was a prideful, elegant walk that screamed, "Hey, world, I'm ready for you! I'm ready to go out there and see what there is to see and do what there is to do. I'm on an adventure!"

That walk has stayed with me my whole life. It was partly because of my strut that I became one of the cool girls in school and hung out with the popular crew. On some level, it helped me to become a performer. I was walking the walk of self-confidence and feeling it. When it came time to release my first album, I was able to resist the pressures to look a certain way, and I created my own style. I called myself "Queen" because that was exactly how I felt inside, and I pulled off the royal African look I created for myself—with the robes, wooden jewelry, and hats—because at seventeen I already had that swagger.

Real Women Have Curves

Of course, there were many times throughout my early career when my confidence was tested. The pressure to lose weight would come and go all through my career, and sometimes it was immense. It hurt when a studio executive told me to slim down, but for the most part I was comfortable in my own skin. I liked my size, and I thought it was ridiculous when our producers told us to lose weight when we were doing *Living Single*. We were supposed to reflect women in the real world, so what sense would it make to viewers if we were all skinny?

The decision to lose weight came much later in life, in 2002, and more for health reasons than anything else. I was at my heaviest when I was playing Matron "Mama" Morton in *Chicago*, and that heft was right for my character. My inspiration was my grandmother Nana Owens, a larger-than-life glamour queen who wore sequins, went on cruises, and owned a gun. My aunts and I inherited her big ol' gazungas, but they held up just fine on Nana, right up until she died at the ripe old age of ninety-four. I was in Toronto filming *Chicago* when that happened, and I was devastated, but her spirit was right there with me. When I did that number "When You're Good to Mama," the scene that earned me an Oscar nomination, the director kept telling me to think of Sophie Tucker, "the Last of the Red Hot Mamas." No disrespect, but it was Nana I could relate to for that part. She gave that character its soul.

That was one long, cold winter in Toronto. By the end of six months, I wasn't feeling my best. I was sluggish. My back hurt. I really wanted to lose weight for my next role. I like to look a bit different for each part I play. But mostly I just wanted to feel better, be healthy, have more energy. I also wanted to go hard and slim down to see if I could reduce my breast size. I was sick of having my bra straps dig into my shoulders all the time. So when I moved back to Los Angeles, I immediately found myself a trainer, Jeannette, who works with me to this day.

When we met, the first thing I did was grab my stomach and say, "There's a lotta love here, and you're gonna have a hard time separating me from all this love!" Jeannette laughed. She was used to training models and actresses—people who were already physically fit but still miserable and dissatisfied with their lives. I was the polar opposite. We did most of our workouts outside and had fun. Jeannette knew fifty exercises I could do with just a park bench, so I never got bored. Over the next six weeks, I trained so intensely—twice a day for at least two hours—I lost twenty-five pounds. My breasts didn't budge, but I felt better, and I reconnected to the athlete in me.

I've been pretty consistent about exercise in my life ever since. Maybe I'm not always as consistent as I should be, but when I go for a few days without it, I don't feel so great about myself. When I was filming *Just Wright* in New York, I made a point of having a big pink bicycle on the set, and I rode it all over the streets of Manhattan. I kept it *moving,* soaking it all in—the pigeons swooping past, the people dodging taxicabs, some driver cursing out another driver. I draw energy from this. It helps me appreciate this great adventure called life.

Every chance I get, I try to exercise. When I work out really hard and pound that treadmill for an hour, I feel beautiful. I take pride in my accomplishment. I like the way I look in my Nike cap, sneakers, and sweats, with my flushed skin and hair that's damp at the roots from sweat. I almost feel more gorgeous in those moments, when I've done something good for myself, than when I'm all glammed up in a designer gown for some awards show.

Exercise and health have become so closely tied to my self-esteem, I've made it a priority. When my body feels good I feel more energized and alive, and that's sexy. I'm taking care of this body God gave me. I'm more careful about what I put in my mouth. My mother's a Southern girl, and I grew up on smoth-ered chicken, collard greens, and home fries. Every-thing has some kind of gravy in it and lots of salt. I eased up on the salt and adapted a few recipes. I love my greens, but now I'll make them with turkey bacon instead of back fat or a ham hock. The Jenny Craig program helped a lot. I try to eat more organic foods, more vegetables, less fat. I'll pass on the second helping of mac and cheese. Comfort food has its place, but no one needs that much comfort, least of all me!

We may not have all been born looking like super-models, but so what? We become beautiful when we do things to take care of ourselves, inside and out. It's not just about how I look, it's about my health and doing things that will let me live longer by keeping down my blood pressure, glucose, and cholesterol.

Health Is Beauty

You've got to maintain. I know women who never miss their weekly appointment at the hair salon, but you'll never catch them sweating it out in the gym. That's like having a car decked out with rims, a nice new sound system, and an expensive paint job, but the engine's dead because you never take it in for a tune-up. Your ride may look great, but it doesn't run, so what's the point?

Nurture what God gave you. We make our worst decisions when we're not feeling our best. We don't see ourselves in the right light, and we hurt ourselves even more. We stay in relationships where we're being abused, we don't go for our real dreams and goals in life, we give pieces of ourselves away that we can never get back, because we don't appreciate who we are and what we have. We tear ourselves down for what we are or are not, instead of celebrating who we are.

But we empower ourselves when we put our health and well-being first. Getting fit doesn't just change your figure, it transforms your attitude. You put yourself up on a higher pedestal. When a woman loses weight, her confidence soars. She doesn't take so much crap from her man. She finds her voice. She expresses herself.

Exercise has become inextricably linked with my self-esteem. The other day I woke up not feeling my best. Ladies, you know what I'm talking about. It happens every twenty-eight days or so. I'd had a long, intense week of promoting my new album, and I was exhausted. I hadn't slept the night before. I didn't want to get out of bed, but I didn't want to be *in* bed. I was in purgatory. I got up, looked at myself in the mirror, and didn't like what I saw. I had a nine a.m. workout session with another trainer, Andrea, and I wanted to cancel. But then I heard Jeannette's voice say, *You can do it, Dana. Just try, and you'll feel better.* She was in New York, but she'd done such a good job of getting into my head, she could be heard from thousands of miles away!

When I got to the gym, I warned Andrea that I wasn't feeling so good. I was crampy and tired. She suggested we just go for a walk. I loved that idea. So we headed out to a nearby park, and after about fifteen minutes the blood started circulating in my body, my vision cleared, and my mood lifted. I feed off what I see around me—dogs running in the park, kids playing, old couples walking hand in hand. I saw one elderly gentleman who was stretching almost to the point of doing splits. He put me to shame! I thought, "Well, this man is twice my age, so if he can walk, I can walk." When I got home later that day and looked at myself in the mirror, I felt a lot better about the person who was staring back at me. I'd worked hard to do something I didn't want to do. I felt a sense of accomplishment. I got out of my own head, moved my body, and made myself feel alive and beautiful again.

I love this body of mine more and more every day. In fact, my friends call me "Naked Girl" because I'm always strutting around the house in the buff, I am so proud of my curves. As I age, it feels like I'm growing into my beauty. I love my smile, my cheekbones, my eyes. But I don't think my beauty lies just in my face. I also love my curves, my genetics, my muscles, my hips. Mine is a grown woman's body, and I love the way it transforms into a more womanly shape. I even like my feet!

Diet and exercise have helped me build this love. I used to wear looser clothes, but in the last few years I've enjoyed wearing those va-voom gowns and waist-cinching dresses and suits that show off my curves and accentuate my booty. I may be a big girl, but I am damn proud of my shape.

There is beauty in every kind of woman, but when people focus on trying to capture one specific look, they miss out on all this variety. They also lose sight of the value of character. But first we have to see it and appreciate it in ourselves.

Beauty Is You

My mother had a great exercise she used to teach the kids in her class at Irvington High School to help them love themselves a little more. Mom would see a lot of very troubled teenagers. So many of these kids were from broken homes. A number of them were abused, sexually and physically. Often these kids would act out, and their grades would suffer. Even though she had forty kids in her class, she made a point of remembering each and every one of them by name in the first week. She also made a point of remembering a little detail about each of the kids so they'd know they were being seen and acknowledged. Often it was the first time they felt noticed in school.

She made them write lists of all the things they liked about themselves, and it would usually stump them. Some kids turned over their papers and started to cry. Ms. O would have to get them started. "Come on, now," she'd say. "You've got a pretty smile, write that down!" Or, "You take care of your brothers and sisters." Or, "You have a great sense of style, you always wear fly clothes."

This one seventeen-year-old girl was so tired and angry because she had to get up every morning to feed her younger siblings breakfast and get them ready for school while her mom was still in bed, too strung out on crack to move. This poor girl couldn't think of anything nice to say about herself, because she'd turned all that bitterness and anger from her unhappy home life in on herself. Eventually, after some coaxing from my mother, she wrote down the only good thing she could think of: "I believe that God loves me and He is going to make things better."

Ms. O would tell these kids to tape their lists to the bathroom mirror. They had to read their lists, those few words of self-love, while they brushed their teeth, to remind themselves how special they were, no matter how rough the day got. And as the school year progressed, those boys and girls walked taller, got better grades, and graduated. Several even went off to college. All because my mother loved them enough to teach them to love themselves.

Speaking of Ms. O, I just remembered another life-stopping moment. It had a bigger impact on my self-esteem than any glamorous photo shoot ever could.

It was my twenty-fourth birthday, and I decided to celebrate by inviting my closest friends to party on a yacht in Marina del Rey. This was around the time I was doing *Living Single*. Something started happening to my face. Up until then, I looked like my dad. Everyone who met him and me together would say, "Wow, you look just like your father," and I didn't mind. I was proud of my dad. He's a handsome guy. But as I was getting dressed for the party, I stepped out onto the balcony to look at the sunset, turned to go back inside, and suddenly caught myself in the mirror. I saw my mother staring back at me.

There was something about the elegant dress I wore that day and the way I was standing at that moment that made me really feel like a woman. I thought, "Wow, look at you!" My mother's beauty was right there, in my reflection. I had her cheekbones, her eyes, her smile. This is the moment we can look forward to as young women growing up and wondering to ourselves, "Am I beautiful?" It's the sudden recognition that, yes, we are.

Unlike her students, I didn't need Mom's bathroom mirror checklist because I could see her face in mine, and that was enough to remind me of all the things I love about myself even beyond my mother's gorgeous face. I saw all the kindness, compassion, and wisdom she had nurtured in me. I saw my soul.

Seeing myself in that moment was the first time I truly felt comfortable in my own skin. I felt like a lady, and that was a good thing.

CHAPTER 3

Money

I could tell something was wrong the second I heard my bookkeeper's voice on the phone. He was an accounting student I'd put in charge of paying all my bills, and somehow, over the last few months, he'd gotten overwhelmed. Using the signature card I gave him, he wrote check after check after check to pay off every bill that came into the office, not even questioning the amounts. Then, just as he was getting ready to pay off another pile of invoices coming due, he noticed something was off.

"Uh, Dana, there's something I have to tell you." It sounded like his stomach was about to fall out of his mouth. "I, uh . . . Okay, I'm just gonna say it. There's no money left in your account."

"Stop playing! That ain't funny."

"No, really. It's gone. Boss, I'm so sorry. . . ."

"Whaaaat?! Are you kidding me? How can that be? What do you mean it's all gone?"

I couldn't believe it. It was the spring of 2000, and I'd been working my butt off down in Los Angeles, doing my talk show and a heap of other projects. I was making plenty of money. This just didn't make sense. Then, seconds after I got off the phone with my bookkeeper, my accountant called.

"Dana, this is bad. There's nothing left in your account, and you owe the IRS one million dollars. Those taxes are due next week!"

I thought I was going to die. I literally was going to lose it. It wasn't the worst life-stopping moment of my life, but it was up there in the top five. I felt nauseated. I couldn't breathe. There wasn't a nickel in my account to pay the IRS, and they don't play. It was a scary situation to be in. I'd been working so hard, and for what? Just like that, I was broke. How was it possible? Who let this happen?

I was mad at everybody. But mostly I was angry at myself. I should have known better. I should have paid more attention to my finances. I should have handled my business and not left everything on the shoulders of some poor kid who was totally out of his depth. It was my fault.

Street Ain't Smart Enough

This is the first time I've talked publicly about going broke. I'm sharing this with you so you'll understand how easy it can be to lose it all at any level of wealth when you're not looking hard enough.

We thought we made all the right moves. Shakim and I had decided a year before to set up our own record company. Both of us could have had a deal with a major label and taken high-level, lucrative jobs as music executives. It would have been easier in a lot of ways. You get expense accounts and travel accounts. You start buying things like flashy cars and houses, and before you know it, you've acquired so much stuff and gotten so used to having everything paid for that you become dependent on that label for everything. You become its slave.

We never wanted to be like that. Shakim and I are the kind of people who want to be free to think out of the box and not have to go through some committee to do it. We'd been managing several successful artists for years through Flavor Unit Management, and we already had a small distribution deal with a record label, but we wanted to take it to the next level. We wanted to be like Jay-Z and Damon Dash at Roc-A-Fella or Baby and Slim at Cash Money Records. We wanted ownership. These guys proved that you could create a high level of success when you own the content of the things you create, whether it's music, movies, or merchandising.

We'd heard the horror stories about what can happen when an artist doesn't read before signing on the dotted line and someone else ends up owning all your publishing and gets all the royalty checks. We didn't want to do all the up-front work and sign our lives away to lawyers and accountants who were making all the real money behind the scenes. We wanted to build our own business and create an independent record label with all these amazing artists we'd found. The numbers didn't lie. You have to pay a small fee to get the record printed up and sent to the stores, but after expenses you can make as much as $10 a record. With minimal success, you can reap lots of benefits.

But we didn't factor in the tremendous overhead and start-up costs. Getting your own business off the ground can be like throwing money into a vast pit. It never ends. And Shakim and I didn't help ourselves. We had way too many employees on our payroll, more than ten, and very few of them were generating enough income to justify their salaries. We were both guilty of being too soft on our employees. We had friends and family members working for us—people we liked and felt deserved a shot—and we wanted to be loyal to them. It was hard for us to separate our emotions from our business.

We threw hundreds of thousands of dollars into our new label. We spent $60,000 to host the Hot 97 Summer Jam and generate some buzz about our artists. We spent thousands more on radio promotion, tours, merchandising, vans, you name it. Instead of buying studio time, which was getting expensive, we decided to buy our own forty-eight-track recording studio. We took over Whitney Houston's old space and called it Millennium Recordings. We redid the whole place. In addition to the main recording studio, it had nice lounges, two pre-production rooms, and a rehearsal space to prepare for touring.

Good Money After Bad

I'm not saying it was a bad investment, but now we were paying for our offices, the studio, way too many employees (including their salaries and benefits), and artists' expenses. And boy, let me tell you, artists can be like thankless children. They are expensive to keep happy, and they have no appreciation or idea of what is being done for them, all before they've even dropped an album. As much as we believed in their talents, they had yet to generate a cent for our label.

Meanwhile, my personal expenses were running high. I had my mom and dad and everyone else I'm looking out for. It was bad for Shakim, too. He put his own skin in the game, even though he had a wife and two kids to support. We were working on finding investors to raise some cash and help us cover our costs until we could generate revenue, but everyone who took to our idea somehow never got around to paying us the money for it. Still, Shakim and I continued to cover the costs, because we believed we'd raise the cash eventually.

Sign Everything

Somehow in the confusion and our zealousness to reach our goal, we weren't thinking clearly and we had overextended ourselves almost to the point of bankruptcy. They were honest mistakes. No one was doing anything wrong. But in a short space of time, my bookkeeper had signed some $500,000 worth of checks out of my account, and I wasn't keeping tabs on any of this.

Then, bam! That phone call. By the time I scraped myself up off the floor, phone still in hand, I knew I had some serious housecleaning to do. I called my mother, and she calmed me down, like she always does. Then I called my accountant, who helped me come up with a plan to pay back the IRS in a way that could be maintained. What happened wasn't his fault, either, because lots of bills weren't going directly to his office. But we had to work out a new system.

Around that time, I remember watching an episode of *Oprah*, where she talked about how you should never let anyone else sign your checks. I thought, "Damn, Oprah, why are you telling me this now?" I closed my account and opened a new one with a zero balance, and now I sign everything. *Everything!* No check is too small. No matter where I am in the world, my accountant prepares the checks, then sends them to me to sign. It's well worth the extra time and effort, because I catch errors no one else would. The other day, I saw a check my offices had cut that was overpaying by more than $20,000. If I'd allowed it to go through uncorrected, that money would be gone forever. It's not like the vendor would be in any hurry to pay back the difference. As if! With a little extra diligence, I'm saving myself thousands of dollars every year.

That wasn't the only change we made. Shakim and I had to take a hard look in the mirror, and at each other, and figure out what our priorities were and where we were going wrong. He told me that running the record label and the management company was too much. He was overwhelmed. He needed a life! We had to choose which side of Flavor Unit would be our focus. We decided to drop all but a couple of the artists we were managing. We were consumed with guilt about this. But guess what? Those artists found new management, and they're thriving today.

It was the same with our employees. I scaled back on my bookkeeper's responsibilities so he could focus on getting his accounting degree at college. We also had to let a couple of people go, and I had a few hard conversations with those who weren't working efficiently enough to justify what we were paying them.

I felt horrible about this. Shakim and I were making emotional decisions about our business and keeping people around out of a sense of loyalty. But we weren't doing ourselves any favors, and we weren't helping our employees to grow, either. Instead, we were creating a bunch of dependents. I'm proud to say that everyone we let go ended up doing just fine on their own. When they realized they weren't going to get that check anymore, they simply figured out their next move, hustled, and found themselves a much better fit. We should have done it a long time ago. All those salaries we were floating could have paid for my nieces' college fees and then some.

Shakim and I totally restructured our business, and it's been great for us both personally and professionally. Our label has been thriving ever since. We've branched into movies, merchandising, and production. We're seeing steady growth just as many major labels are teetering on the brink of disaster. Had we gone that route, our gravy train would have reached the end of the line by now. We're both still a little too softhearted when it comes to employees and the occasional venture with friends, but for the most part we've been able to separate our feelings from our finances.

School Yourself

I also made a point of educating myself on the subject of personal wealth. A lot of us weren't raised to know why one type of savings account is better than another. Shakim and I got on-the-job training. Life has been our college, and sometimes we had to learn the hard way. But if we'd been more proactive about getting our hands on the right information, we could have avoided a lot of pain.

I went to the bookstore, as I often like to do, and browsed the shelves. There weren't too many offerings catering specifically to women, which is why I decided to write this chapter. Somehow, money isn't supposed to be something women worry about. But one title did catch my eye: Suze Orman's *The 9 Steps to Financial Freedom*. Several captions in the table of contents spoke to me. I started reading it right there in the bookstore. She writes about all kinds of things that never even occurred to me, but made perfect sense. Even the fact that you should keep all the bills nicely folded and organized in your wallet, not crumpled up and scattered all over the place. It's a small, simple thing, but it's about something bigger: taking care of the money that takes care of you and not taking it for granted. Wealth is a blessing from God, and it needs to be handled with respect on all levels.

Eventually I bought the book, took it home, and made copious notes about insurance policies, living wills, trusts, how to save, and which 401(k)s, annuities, and IRAs would be best for me. I called my accountant and grilled him about all these financial products I'd only vaguely understood before. I was determined to reach a level of financial sophistication. Nothing less than my future was at stake. I thought long and hard about my financial goals. I don't want to work this hard when I'm sixty-five. I want to kick back and enjoy life, knowing I've taken care of my family and built a legacy for the children I hope to have one of these days.

I wouldn't wish that phone call on anyone. But as frightening as that going broke moment was, I feel like God was trying to tell me something. Often in church, the pastor says that God is going to give you only what you can handle. He's not trying to put money in the pockets of people who haven't gotten to a place where they can take care of it. He wants to bless you, and He wants you to make the most of His blessings. I think He wanted to bless me even more, but He also wanted me to wake up and pay attention to what was really going on.

Quality of Life

This isn't just about materialism. For me, affluence doesn't represent fancy cars, nice houses, jewelry, and all the toys. Sure, I enjoy these things, but they don't define me. I care more about the financial security that wealth brings, to me and to my family. I want to be debt-free. I want to be able to provide for the people I love, as well as myself, and ensure that I have the freedom to do things for my spirit and not just for my pocketbook. I want to be able to travel, pursue creative projects that aren't necessarily commercial, and support causes I care about, like education for inner-city kids. Accumulating personal wealth and taking control of your financial future is about empowerment, not stuff.

This last recession just proves to me that we as individuals have to pay more attention. With all the greed on Wall Street and crooks like Bernie Madoff allowed to run wild with our investments and gamble our futures away, we can't afford to be passive about our finances anymore. I know plenty of people who had millions and lost it all because they gave up control to so-called investment experts, money managers, accountants, and lawyers and got robbed. By not paying attention, they cheated themselves.

I've made similar mistakes. It was a steep learning curve for me. I have a semester of college, and I'm street smart, but money came to me at a very young age, before I'd acquired any real investment savvy. I had some of the basics down. My mother opened an account for my brother and me at the Howard Savings Bank (which no longer exists) and taught us both how to write a check—something many adults in our community never learned how to do. Every week, we'd set aside some of our allowance and put it in the bank. Every birthday and Christmas, our grandmother, my mom's mom, Katherine Bray, would send us a crisp new five-dollar bill (come to think of it, Nana Bray still does). That wasn't money to blow; I might have taken out a dollar or two to buy candy, but we stashed most of it into our savings account. And I continued that saver mentality all through my teens.

My dad also taught us some valuable lessons about how to manage a buck. When I was ten, my mom was away on a trip and we were staying with our father near downtown Newark. Dad was working double shifts, so we were basically latchkey kids, which was pretty common in those days. To keep us entertained, Dad would give us $10 and send us off to the center of town to spend the afternoon exploring all the toy shops and dollar stores. That money was to pay for lunch and a drink and bus fare, depending on how far up the street we got.

We had a blast. It was my dad's way of teaching us financial independence. He wanted to see how frugal we could be. Ten dollars could buy you a lot in a dime store thirty years ago, and he was interested to see what kinds of choices we were making about our spending.

Long Ass Week

I remember getting my first paycheck. I was fifteen, and I found a job at Burger King while I was still in school. I really wanted that job. There were plenty of fun summer jobs kids could take working in parks and day camps, but this was serious work, plus I'd get free food. I did everything from working the cash register to cleaning the toilets. I made $88.46 that first week. I remember because I knew exactly how many hours I'd worked, and I was shocked by how much of my money went back to "the Man." Taxes, Social Security—everyone had to take their cut. I had to ask my mother, "What's FICA?" "Where did all my money go?" I gave my mom a couple of bucks, bought myself a mix tape, and put what was left in my savings account. It wasn't much, but it felt good, because it was money I earned through my own hard work.

Two years later, the circumstances couldn't have been more different. I wasn't even signed to a label yet and my first record, "Princess of the Posse," was playing on the radio. I got my first big check, a few thousand dollars, and I blew quite a bit of it. I even bought gold teeth! My brother and I used to try out these hip-hop looks that were big at the time, with all the chains and tooth grills, but between us we had only one gold chain, which we had to share, and the rest we had to improvise with gold foil. But gold teeth? It was ridiculous! I didn't even get proper ones made at the dentist. I bought them at a jewelry store in the mall. They were the kind you just snap on. Needless to say, they disappeared within a couple of days. Money down the drain.

When I was nineteen, I went back to my more responsible ways. I'd just released my first album on

Tommy Boy Records, *All Hail the Queen*. I had four or five singles out, and Shakim and I were having quite the ride. We were on tour and making first $1,000, then $2,000, then $5,000 a show. We tried handling all our finances ourselves, sending a third to my mother after our expenses and putting the rest in our account, but eventually it got to be too much. We found an accountant at a big, reputable firm in Manhattan to manage our expenses. We thought we were straight, but one day we went to his office to meet with him and he told us there was no money left in our account.

We were furious. I wanted to kill this guy. How could it be that an accountant—someone who is educated and gets paid extremely well to provide a professional service—would not at least notify us when funds were getting low? It made no sense. But as history would later prove, we had a lot more to learn. When it comes to your own money, you can't assume anything. Even accountants have to be held accountable. Over the next few years, we went through a couple more accountants who were mediocre at best. Our current guy is great. He's professional and honest. But we don't just leave him to it. We treat our relationship more like a partnership and talk with him regularly about the state of our finances. We no longer let anything slide.

Money Matters

This isn't about greed. Handling your business and taking care of your money is an important part of loving yourself. Too often we live in denial about our money situation. We don't want to face it. We make emotional decisions about how we spend, maxing out our credit cards to buy shoes to make ourselves feel good. But it never works because the problem we're trying to cover up is still there. Meanwhile, we've buried ourselves deeper in the hole. That's not how a queen treats herself. Sure, she'll go on a shopping spree now and then if she can afford it. But she gets her money straight first, because she knows there's a lot more at stake than grabbing the latest "It" bag off the shelf. Financial security frees you up to take better care of mind, body, and soul.

Of course, it's different if you've got children and you're struggling to put food on the table and a roof over their heads. It doesn't get more real than that. My heart goes out to families that are facing financial hardship, especially in this recession. But even when you think you have nothing, if you educate yourself, you will learn that there are small things you can do to stretch a dollar and set aside a little money to save. You don't have to be a slave to credit card companies and those crazy interest rates. There's no need to take out a mortgage you can't afford and end up in the streets because your home went into foreclosure. Ladies, you've got to own your crown outright—don't pay for it through some extortionate layaway plan!

When I was growing up, my mother drummed into me the importance of financial independence. She didn't want to see me end up stuck in a bad relationship and dependent on some man for my survival. We knew too many women in our community who were trapped. They got married and had babies, and when their man started cheating, drinking, or being abusive, they didn't know where to turn or where to even start. They had to find a job with no experience and no two nickels to rub together. There's nothing wrong with being a homemaker, if the marriage stays strong and your husband is able to be a good provider. But that's just not the way I was raised.

The Best Things in Life . . .

Both of my parents always worked. My father was a cop, and my mom had a job as a secretary even when my brother and I were babies. Thursday must have been payday for my dad, because I remember we always got dressed up and went to a nice Chinese restaurant for dinner, and sometimes caught a movie afterward. But Mom and Dad invented all these other ways to have fun that didn't cost a thing. Sometimes we'd drive to a nice neighborhood to look at the houses and enjoy the peace and quiet. Or my mother would pack up a picnic and we'd drive to some nearby park, set up the blankets and a tent, and pretend we were out on some adventure in the wilderness. Or we'd fry some chicken, make up some potato salad and Kool-Aid, and drive to the Jersey shore for the day. Or my dad would take my brother and me fishing or camping in the woods. It was all free, and these things gave me some of my happiest childhood memories.

When my parents separated and Dad moved out, my mother could no longer afford to live in the garden apartment in Hillside we were renting, so we moved to the projects. Mom was too proud and independent to ask her family back home in Maryland for support, so she made sacrifices. But she had a plan. She went back to college to get a teaching degree. In between classes, she worked three jobs. She was a waitress and a maid at the Holiday Inn. She worked as a janitor, and she put in hours on the loading dock of the local post office, lifting boxes until she injured her back. She earned enough money to send us to Catholic school, feed and clothe us. A year later, she even saved enough to put toward a down payment on a small house on Littleton Avenue, far away from the projects.

That whole time, we felt rich because our lives were full and interesting. Mom researched all the fun, educational stuff we could do for free or for just a few dollars. She took us to museums. She found us piano lessons at a community center for $3.00. She exposed us to other cultures and ideas. She even decorated our tiny apartment tastefully, so it felt like a real home. We had no money, but as I child I never once felt deprived.

Even today, I don't live and die by how much money I have. An expensive pair of sneakers, the nicest car, the latest clothes—these things are not necessities. Sure, I enjoy having money and I like to spend every now and then, but often we get caught up in the excesses. Instead, we have to be appreciative of what we do have.

I can't fathom why someone would blow his brains out over losses in the stock market. Greed makes no sense to me. That's someone who loves money more than life. I've been watching a lot of CNN lately, and you hear all these horror stories on the news about what the recession is doing to families. One guy lost his job and all his savings on Wall Street. He had bills up to his neck, and his house was about to go into foreclosure. And nobody knew. His response was to kill his wife and children, then himself. That was a person who was so spiritually empty, so full of despair, that losing all the material things in life made him think his only option was to annihilate himself and his whole family. He couldn't see the positive things in his life—even the fact that he had a family who loved him or the knowledge that everyone was healthy. He couldn't feel the joy of simply living another day. And a lot of people get like that.

During the tough times, you have to reach out and attach yourself to something beyond the material. For some, that might be the Bible, the Torah, or the Koran. Or maybe you just need to read a self-help book or listen to some tape that gives you positive affirmation. Whatever it is, it's out there, and those words of hope are free.

For me, it's also about looking at those who are less fortunate than you are. Sometimes you just have to change your perspective. In *The Art of Happiness*, His Holiness the Dalai Lama talks about a man who was distraught because he made $40,000 a year and was convinced he didn't have enough money to make ends meet for his family. Then he met someone who had the same number of mouths to feed on just $20,000. It completely changed the way he viewed his own situation. No matter how bad it gets, there's always someone worse off than you. Appreciating that fact makes you more thankful, no matter what your situation.

Enrich Your Soul

Giving back is another great way to change up the way you see things. Throughout my life I've found that whenever I'm going through certain changes or I feel down about certain things, giving makes me feel better, despite my situation. It might be writing a big check for a cause I care about or giving someone my time. There are a lot of causes that matter to me and many more I want to be involved in.

It enriches me to know that my dollars may have gotten someone in Africa medication for HIV and prolonged a life or rescued a child prostitute off the streets of Cambodia. Even just doing our annual toy drive for kids in our community brings such joy to me, my mother, and Shakim. Knowing I've made a difference in some small way, I get so much more than I give. It's almost like a gift to myself.

Education is another cause that is extremely important to me. Through the Lancelot H. Owens Scholarship Foundation we started in my brother's name, my mother and I give out scholarships and other forms of financial support to inner-city kids so they can go to college. But even if it's not a full scholarship, we'll give a needy child money for books or enough to pay for lunches for a month. We give what we can. Kids are our future, and we don't invest in them enough. Not equally, anyway. I treasure the fact that when you give a child an education, you allow him or her the freedom to dream and to become an amazing person, because now that child has the knowledge and ability to go out and learn more and create. That person you helped to educate may come back and help another kid. It moves us all forward.

Give to Get

There are times when I will write a check for $20,000 or $50,000 or $100,000, but if you took a peek at my expenses or the number on my bank account, you would say, "Girl, you better hold on to that!" But when you give, you get back in multiples. Of course, you have to treat your money with respect and manage it with care, but cash comes and goes, and you can always make more. I've never regretted giving money away to someone who is less fortunate. I give it with freedom, knowing that what I am really doing is giving myself a gift. The feeling I might get from buying a new car just doesn't stack up to the knowledge that I may have helped a little girl in Asia who was raped because some guy thought her virginity would cure him of AIDS.

I can't wait to go to Cambodia to visit the girls rescued from a life of prostitution by Somaly Mam. This woman, a former victim of sexual slavery herself, has built a safe haven for young girls she risked her life to pull out of those situations. We were both being honored by *Glamour* magazine a couple of years ago, and I had to follow Somaly after she gave her acceptance speech. I was so moved by her story, I wrote her organization a check for $150,000 on the spot. Some of that money, as well as some cash from Barbara Walters, helped build a vocational school and home outside Phnom Penh where the girls could live in safety and learn how to sew and cut hair. Outside this modest building, embedded in a small garden, there are two fancy plaques with our names written in gold. The contrast between these shiny black marble markers and their humble surroundings is touching. Gold Grammy statues are always nice, but knowing that this tribute exists in my name halfway around the world, in a dusty corner of Southeast Asia I've never even seen, means more to me than any industry award.

But giving doesn't have to be on such a grand

scale. If you pass a homeless person who is hungry and doesn't have anywhere to sleep that night, and all you have is a couple of bucks in your pocket, you can still put a coin in his cup and feel good about that. You don't even have to spend money to give. Sometimes giving is just a simple act of kindness. I'm the type of person who will help an old lady across the street or stop when someone's pulled over by the side of the road with a flat tire. Giving can just be talking to one of my younger cousins, nieces, or nephews and offering them some advice or support. Taking the time to just listen can make a huge difference in someone's life.

Try to incorporate giving into your life as much as possible. Even if it's just taking the time to have a quick conversation with a stranger. The other day I was in a Blimpie getting a platter together for my mother's church. They were having a choir rehearsal after work and people come in hungry, so my mother likes to bring something. A couple of girls were shocked to see Queen Latifah at a Blimpie, and one of them asked for my autograph. I was happy to oblige. It was a small thing, but to her it was huge. She said, "You don't know how much this means to me. I was really having a bad day, and you just made my day!"

It was really that simple. You don't know what's going on in someone else's world, so you have to try to be as nice as possible. You never know what kind of impact you can have on that person's life with a small act of kindness. You don't have to go around giving autographs, but just asking someone how they're doing and showing you care can make a difference, especially during hard times. A little compassion can go a long way.

There's so much more to life than chasing a dollar. Yes, money's important, and you have to respect it. I learned that lesson the hard way. But I don't want to live my life on a hamster wheel, making more money to make more money to buy more stuff. It's just stuff, and like I learned when I lost my gold tooth in two days, you can't afford to get too attached to material objects. They don't define you. If you take away my cars and my houses, I will still be the same person. My dogs, Isis and Sing Sing, will still love me. I will still have my closest friends and family. And I will still be able to enjoy a beautiful sunset or a walk by the sea and so many other things that you can't put a price tag on. Mom and Dad taught me well.

I know it's been tough for many of you. Maybe you're a single mom who's facing foreclosure. Maybe you lost your job and you don't know what to do next. Maybe you can't go to the college you were hoping for because a parent lost a job and the college fund has to go toward paying the bills. Maybe you have a child who's sick and you've run out of health insurance. These days, everyone in America has either been touched by the recession or knows someone who's going through some kind of hardship. You're not alone.

All I can tell you from my own experience is that valleys don't last forever. They really don't. Life has its peaks, its valleys, and its plains, too. And none of them is going to last forever. It's all about persevering through that time and how you handle yourself through those valleys. That's why you need a connection with something higher and deeper than a dollar. Money alone won't sustain you. Have faith that things *will* get better. Look out for yourself, but also know that God is going to look out for you. He has your back, and somehow, some way, He will provide.

CHAPTER 4

Love

Even when you don't think you have it, it's there.
—RITA BRAY OWENS

Everything was neatly and conveniently packed in boxes. We were planning to move from our housing project in Newark, New Jersey. While my brother and I were in school and my mother was at work, a truck pulled up to the door of our unit and everything we had was loaded up. There was just one problem: These weren't movers. Some lowlifes from the neighborhood knew we were leaving, and they helped themselves. They took everything we owned— all the belongings that my mother worked so hard to buy for us so we would have a comfortable home. All our toys, books, electronics, artwork—gone. It was broad daylight, people were watching what was going on, and nobody did a damn thing about it. It was like someone had stamped and sealed one final insult to a life we were leaving behind for good. Now we were really starting fresh.

Not of the Projects

My mother protected my brother and me from a lot of what was going on in Hyatt Court. I was eight when we moved there, but Mom kept telling us, "You may live in the projects, but you're not *of* the projects." We were clear about the fact that the situation was temporary. For my family and me, Hyatt Court wasn't a place to settle down; it was a place you strove to get out of! My mother was determined that we wouldn't get locked in that ghetto mentality that infects so many inner-city children when they feel their situation is hopeless. When school was out, she'd take us down to Virginia to spend the summer with her family, so we would see there was a life outside our immediate environment. She took us to museums, encouraged us to read, and worked three jobs to send us to private Catholic school, where it was safe and the academic standards were high.

But other people in the projects *hated* her for doing this. They thought we thought we were too good for everybody else. They saw my mother send us to school every day in our little uniforms, with our white shirts all crisp and freshly pressed, and said to themselves, "Who does this woman think she is? Does she think she's better than us?" To her face, they called her a "snooty yellow bitch." Not the immediate neighbors, because they got to know my mom somewhat, but the ones who saw her from a distance. They didn't like the fact that my mother was just passing through. Even though my mother was scrubbing toilets to make ends meet, people assumed she had a silver spoon in her mouth. They resented her for wanting a better life for her kids.

She promised to move us out of there within the year, and she delivered in just eleven months. She worked her ass off to get it done. That Christmas, my mother took extra shifts to earn enough money to buy us presents so we wouldn't feel deprived. She hid our toys, already gift-wrapped, in the trunk of her car so we'd be surprised Christmas morning. But somebody must have seen her doing this, because they gave my mother her own nasty surprise. They broke into the car on Christmas Eve and took it all. So during our short year in the projects, we were robbed not once, but *twice*.

Our previous home was in a quiet area outside of Newark. So when we first moved to Hyatt Court, my brother and I saw adventure everywhere. I'd say, "Look, Winki, smokestacks!" My brother would say,

"Oooh, 'sis, I wonder what's over by those train tracks! Let's go find out!" We were fascinated by all the activity going on in the courtyard. We wanted to know what all those kids were doing over in the corner. No wonder my mother was always trying so hard to keep us occupied!

But you'd never know anything was wrong. Mom never complained. She was always pleasant to everyone. She'd say, "Good morning," when she passed someone on the stairs on her way to work, and, "Have a pleasant evening," to whomever she saw on her way back home. Never "How ya doin'?" or "Whaassuup!" Rita Bray Owens was, is, and always will be a lady, and she wasn't about to drop her standards just to fit in.

"You persevere," Mom said. "You don't hold your head down and become part of the problem. You hold your head up and keep on moving."

My Mother's Voice

This is Mom's chapter, and it's all about love. I'm sharing this moment in her life with you because it says so much about who she is. It's the strength of character I see in my mother that makes me who I am today. I know I'm blessed to have a role model like her in my life. She always had my best interests at heart.

The generations that went before us have lived, and they know a thing or two that we don't. Respect that, and take all the wisdom you can from the loving heart of your mother or, if she's no longer in your life like that, any worthy maternal figure in your life—be it a mentor, teacher, older sister, or true friend.

We can't do it all alone. We can rise up only when we stand on the shoulders of those who went before us. You need an older, wiser person in your life to give you advice, support, and strength. We all need someone who will listen and care, with no agenda. Our moms can see the beauty and potential that we can't always see in ourselves, and we need to be open to their unconditional love to help us as we struggle to accept who we are.

My mother showed me what's possible by doing. Her life was hard, but she never claimed to be a victim. As a single mother, she worked around the clock to put herself through college to become an art teacher and give her two children a better life. She clipped coupons and made personal sacrifices to make sure we got a good education. She made sure our home was always well kept, no matter where we lived. She stretched out every meal and used every resource she had to make sure we never felt deprived.

My brother and I didn't have everything we wanted, but we got everything we needed.

But it was the nurturing she gave to our souls that made me who I am today. As an artist with a passion for beauty and self-expression, my mother taught us about primary colors, took us to museums, and kept books around the house with artwork by Salvador Dalí and Romare Bearden. She brought home culture magazines and *The New York Times*. She took us to plays and musicals, always making sure we knew there was a bigger world beyond our four corners in Newark. My mother encouraged me to make up songs, dance, bang on stuff, and do whatever I could to be creative. She gave me my prized possession—the small eight-track cassette player that sat in the middle of my small bedroom. Our home was always filled with music, love, and joy.

Caring to Listen

Her greatest gift to us was her willingness to always listen. Mom took the time to get to know my brother and me as individuals. Even as babies, we weren't just little creatures to be cared for. She was curious about who we were. As the middle child between five brothers and two sisters growing up on army bases in

Maryland, my mother got lost. She blossomed later in life than most because as a kid she didn't quite know who she was. But she was determined to bring out our best selves from an early age. She'd get down at eye level and talk *to* us, not *at* us. When we misbehaved, which was often, she didn't yell. She's soft-spoken and gentle, and I've never known her to raise her voice.

But she made sure we knew when we were wrong. She was clear about the rules, and the worst feeling in the world was knowing we'd disappointed her. She had the same effect on some of her roughest students at Irvington. She made those kids want to excel. Mom—Mamma O or Ms. O to the kids in her class—always had a way of instilling in you the desire to please her and meet her highest expectations, and that's a powerful thing.

Today, my mother is the most precious person in my world. She is my best friend and my greatest ally. She helps me run my management and production company, Flavor Unit. She's in charge of the day-to-day business of our scholarship program, the Lancelot H. Owens Scholarship Foundation. She provides inspiration for many of my acting roles, especially when the character I am playing is feminine but strong. There's a lot of my mother in August from *The Secret Life of Bees*—this gentle, educated woman who takes care of the people she loves.

Whenever I decide I'm going to try something new, Mom's the one in my corner, encouraging me to take the leap. Even when she's afraid for me, she doesn't try to hold me back. She understands I have to take risks, make my own mistakes, and do me. And I always know I'm going to get honest feedback from her. She knows I don't need another fan.

When I did my first jazz album, *Trav'lin' Light*, I asked her advice about rerecording the song "Poetry Man," because I knew it was her favorite. I was nervous, but Mom said I should go for it, and I was giddy when she told me how much she loved what I did. There's always going to be that little kid in me who wants her mother's approval.

How to Live

The best part of having Rita Bray Owens in my life is watching the way she treats each day as a gift. She just turned sixty, and on her birthday she saw her first hockey game and took her first yoga class. She's learning tai chi, and she started piano lessons because she has a big ol' grand piano in her living room and she decided she wanted to be able to play it. Next on her list is dancing lessons. Mom is a young soul who loves being a work in progress, and the day she stops learning, growing, and discovering is the day she stops living.

My mother has a wood carving in the entranceway of her house in New Jersey. It says simply, "LIVE." She looks at it every day to remind herself. She really studies it. She asked me, "Have you ever noticed that if you read 'live' backwards it spells 'evil'? Because to not live, to do the opposite and waste this life God gave us, would be evil." To live—that's her creed.

Mom is the reason why, as I approach forty, I'm not afraid of growing older. She's a perfect example of how to age gracefully and stay vital. Her life is in full flower. For the first time since she and my father divorced, my mother has found a good man, Bobby, a former police officer and the guy who heads up security for the mayor's office in Newark. My mother wasn't looking. She was too busy living her life, and in so doing, *he* found *her*. Now she's planning her wedding. She decided to take her time in finding a life partner, and she didn't mind being single one bit. Her independence was too precious to give up until she found the man who truly deserves her.

Not everyone has a mother who's still around, and some mother/daughter relationships are full of tension. I can understand how hard that must be. I've always had my mother to turn to. She was always there to comfort and advise me, without ever passing judgment. And my world is filled with many other amazing female role models—my mother's mother, Katherine Bray, is eighty-one and still active in the community. Nana must make some forty pound cakes a year for her church bake sales, neighbors' birthdays, funerals. She still drives, hangs out with her church lady friends, and keeps a clean house with pots on the stove simmering something delicious for all the children and grandchildren who come to visit.

Nana Owens, my father's mother, was another important maternal figure in my life. Street smart, tough, glamorous, and fun loving, Nana loved life until the end. Another powerhouse personality, my aunt Elaine Owens, was also a huge influence in my life. She was the one who showed my mother the ropes when she wasn't much more than a child herself, struggling to take care of a newborn and a toddler. Mom had just moved up to New Jersey with my father. She was from the South and didn't know a soul, so Aunt Elaine took her under her wing. These were women who *knew* it takes a village. It was how they lived.

Someone to Lean On

If you can, find a nurturing relationship with an older, wiser female, like an aunt, godparent, grandparent, or friend and grab hold of it. Open yourself up to their love. If you haven't found it yet, it's probably there, coming from some unexpected place. Maybe it's an old schoolteacher, a neighbor, or a friend. Maybe it's not even a female figure in your life. Maybe it's your father or a male friend or relative. You may not think anyone has your back, but someone does. Someone is willing to be there for you. Someone *will* listen. It's up to you to let that person in.

Meanwhile, I'm setting aside the rest of this chapter to loan out my own mother to you, to share some of her own moments and spread the love. Mamma O will take it from here . . .

RITA BRAY OWENS

I think what my Dana is saying is that you are not alone. Even when you think you are, or you are convinced that no one understands you, there's always going to be someone watching and caring. You are loved, and the decisions you make will have a ripple effect on all of the people in your world. Good or bad, your actions will have an impact on the lives of those around you, because you matter.

I've been blessed. I come from a long, unbroken chain of love through the generations. My mother, my mother's mother, and my great-grandmother were all a big part of my life when I was a little girl. Granny and her mother were housemaids in white households in the South. In fact, my mother grew up in the home where her mother, who was unmarried, worked as part of the household staff. My mother was raised alongside the white children who lived there, and they treated her like family.

The only time my mother felt different from her white brothers and sisters was when they went to school. There was still segregation back then, so my mother had to be bused out to a separate school for black children. It bothered her a lot. That's why education became so important to her. She was married and pregnant by seventeen, but she and my father, a military man, still made sure they got their high school diplomas, even in the middle of struggling to raise a young family. So for us, education was non-negotiable. If we had free time, we were expected to go to the library and read. Anything to broaden our horizons. It was imperative that we excelled in school. Every night before dinner, we had to sit at that table and do our homework, and if we didn't have any, my father could care less. Sergeant Bray would give you his own homework assignment, and you could be sure it would be a lot harder than anything the teacher could dish out!

Life in our home was strict. With seven children and

my father often posted far away from all of us for long periods of time, we each had to pull our own weight and contribute to the chores. With just my mother and grandmother to care for us and make ends meet on my father's small salary, our home had to function with maximum efficiency. Responsibilities were parceled out to each child, and even the youngest among us understood how important our roles were. We knew we were a part of the success of the house until Daddy came home a year from now or whenever the army decided.

Bubbles of Love

But there was so much love. As strict as my mother, father, and grandmother were, they never yelled at us. For us, the knowledge of disappointing our parents was far worse than any punishment they could deliver. That bubble of love I lived in protected me from a lot of what was happening in the world around me. Whenever my mother and father got to be in the same country together, they never fought. Voices were never raised, towards each other or towards their children. They were always loving and respectful. I got to see how a man should behave as both a husband and a father. It was a good benchmark to keep filed away in the back of my mind.

We were a tight-knit family. We had our own little community within a community, living in the protected environment of an army base. I was so sheltered. My life consisted of friends, family, school, and church. I'd heard about racism in the abstract, but I was never really exposed to it in a direct way on the various army bases where we lived. Then one hot summer day when I was about eleven, I left the base to walk to the local swimming pool a mile or two away. A group of white guys driving down the street in a Chevy rolled down the window and yelled, "Go home, nigger!"

That was a life-stopping moment for me. I was petrified. And confused. I didn't do anything wrong, and I didn't know those people. Why did they hate me? It shook me to my core. I ran home, crying. The ugliness of it was like a physical shock. My father dried my tears and explained that there were two kinds of people in the world: the ignorant and the educated. He took me to the library and enlightened me about my African-American heritage. He gave me the courage to never let the violence and aggression of other people's hateful language and gestures change who I was or infect me with anger. Hatred was their problem, not mine.

The foundation I had from my parents and grandparents, being part of a generational pattern that was encouraging, nurturing, and loving, stayed with me, even at times in my life when I felt lost. That kind of love and example has real power that can't be underestimated, because it gets passed on to your children and your children's children.

Broken Chains

These days, I see so many examples of how that chain is broken. Kids feel isolated, often with single mothers, not even welfare moms, working long hours and struggling to survive. Their role models are their peers; their influences are whatever dangerous garbage they see on the Internet or whatever the alpha boy or girl in their crowd tells them they should be doing. When I saw more and more pregnant teenage girls in my school, I was disturbed but not surprised, because they're just following the pattern of their own mothers and fathers and whatever they see around them. They have no guidance—no one to be living examples and teach them right from wrong. I still marvel when I meet gems and pearls in my classroom—young men and women who are incredible human beings, despite coming from broken homes. All they need is a little love and guidance to break them out of a bad cycle.

Even with the stability of my wonderful family, I sort of fell through the cracks. I was very much the middle child, and artistically inclined, so that put me in a weird place. As an army brat, moving from base to base, I felt even more isolated. I was always having to pick up and make new friends. I retreated further and further into myself and my fantasy world, focusing on nature and beauty, painting and creating wherever I could. My father recognized this. My parents would buy me paints and brushes for Christmas and birthdays, and whenever my father wrote letters to me from Germany, he'd make his own beautiful drawing for me. Through his own talent, he showed this unspoken appreciation for my artistic side. I remember those letters so poignantly.

There was potential inside me that needed to be tapped. And yet I went straight from being Sergeant Bray's daughter to the wife of Lance Owens, a dashing young soldier in the Honor Guard, fresh from his tour of duty in Vietnam. We met at a little service club in Arlington, Virginia, where my father was based at the time, and I didn't know what hit me. I had acceptances from Howard University and Spelman College, but I gave it all up to move up north to New Jersey and be with my husband. Like my mother when she started having children, I was little more than a child myself when I fell pregnant. I was just an innocent and un-worldly country girl. I plugged straight into Lance's net-work of female family members—his mother and his sister Elaine—and I thank God every day for them. I didn't know a soul in Newark, and as a young mother I was too far away from my own mother to lean on her for support.

Lost in the Cracks

But I really did disappear for a while. My role as wife and mother had overtaken my life. It was only when my husband and I divorced, some ten years later, that I really got to know who Rita was. That's one reason why, to this day, I don't like being referred to as Queen Latifah's mom, aka "the Queen Mother." I fought so long and so hard for my own identity. I'm Rita Bray Owens, Ms. O, Mamma O, teacher, artist, proud mother, and many other things besides—things that I'm still in the process of discovering.

Studying, going to conferences, plays, galleries, exploring new ideas, and discovering the artist in me again was an awakening. At Kean College, where I got my teaching degree, I found mentors and benefited from their brilliance. I met Dr. Elaine Raichle, who saw my potential and believed in it before I did. And Mary Jane Austin, an art education administrator who encouraged me in my creativity and always made me aim higher. I saw how successful, strong, and independent women of my generation could become, particularly in a nurturing community of educated and enlightened individuals.

Every child starts out in life with that potential and the self-confidence to realize it. But then life tears them down. They get distracted and lose their way. I've been through a lot of what these kids are going through now. I was also a teenage mother. I know how hard that is. I've made my own share of mistakes. I've lost my way. But I went through what I went through for a reason. Because when they say, "Ms. O, you don't understand!" I can say, "Oh yes, I do!"

I'm an adult who's navigated through this crazy

thing called life, and talking to the younger generation about the things they should be looking out for on their own journey is the right thing to do. That's why I wanted to teach. To repair some of those broken links in the chain. To look at each individual child in my classroom and make him or her feel like they've really been seen.

Fixing the Links

Sometimes that's all it takes. Just noticing someone, and talking to them like a person of value, can make a huge difference in their lives. My kids were so shocked when I'd remember some incidental detail about what they did or said, like a pair of shoes they wore the week before or an interest they showed in a particular period of art. Half the time they couldn't even believe I remembered their names, the classrooms at Irvington High were so rowdy and overcrowded. When I remembered one girl's name in the first few days of the new school year, she asked me, "How do you do that, Ms. O?" I said, "Because I love you!" She was so giddy and embarrassed. It's a word a lot of these kids don't get to hear very often. They're used to being just someone's pain in the butt. So I made it a point of telling them every day.

My classroom became a sanctuary for those children. But out in the hallways it was another story. As an educator, I can't tell you how many times I had to walk down the hallway and ask, "Is there a problem?" This one boy had his girlfriend jacked up against a locker, getting ready to smack the daylights out of her. Even girls would brutalize each other, fighting over a man! And over the years, it got worse. Our nice middle-class community got fractured by drugs, poverty, and the isolation of immigrant families struggling to adjust to a new culture. Kids from Haiti and the Dominican Republic didn't know where they fit. Bright students in their own countries, they had to suffer the humiliation of being put back a couple of grades here because there was a language barrier. Girls and boys joined cliques and gangs, usually divided up along ethnic and racial lines, so they felt like they belonged somewhere. But it never solved the problem. Instead it created an unhealthy outlet for rage and violence.

Some of these kids have so much anger inside them. They want to fight each other all the time for the slightest thing, even if it's just a kid accidentally brushing past another down the hallway. But the rage is not just about that fight over something trivial they're about to have. It's about their father who's never there for them, or their mother who's been bringing home a string of no-good boyfriends, and all those things that are happening in their world that they feel helpless to correct.

It got so bad in the Irvington High community that several students had become homeless, and they were faking it so they could stay in school and graduate. More and more, my students were coming to me with overwhelming problems. They'd say, "Ms. O, can I talk to you?" I'd say, "You need to talk to me right this minute?" They'd say, "Uh-huh." I'd invite them into my "office"—a broom closet, but it did nicely for these purposes. In the privacy of that little room, they'd tell me about some school bully who had plans to beat their heads in after school. Girls would talk about boy-friends pressuring them into all kinds of unthinkable situations, like having group sex with their friends for money. Boys and girls would talk about being smacked around and sexually abused at home. When it was that bad, and laws were being broken, we'd take certain steps to intervene. Most of the time they already knew in their hearts the right thing to do, but they needed someone to listen to them without judgment, so they could think through the situation without the noise and pressure that existed outside that closet door. You've got to give yourself some space and time to quietly con-template, and if you can find a wise, neutral third party to give you some perspective, even better. We should all remember that when making our own vital deci-sions. It might save your life.

The key is to be gentle. Young women, and men, have fragile self-esteem, and they get knocked down plenty already by their parents and their peers. Some of these students dress so raw. Girls get especially wrong-headed notions about what to wear to be part of the cool crowd. One young lady in particular caught my attention in the hallway. She wasn't in my class, but you couldn't help but notice her because she was a big girl who was busting out of her blouse. Even worse, she had *on a miniskirt that was so short, you could see the color of her underwear. As she headed up the staircase, I caught up to her and whispered, "I just wanted you to know that everyone has a full view underneath that skirt of yours, especially when they get behind you going up the stairs."*

She looked shocked. "Ms. O, I didn't know. Nobody told me!"

I was worried that if she didn't adjust her dress sense, it could set her up for a heap of trouble, so I said, "Girl, you blessed back there! You don't need to be too revealing, because you already have those beautiful curves. Bring the hemline down an inch or two and be a little more mysterious. You got plenty going on. You don't need to be trying that hard!"

"Oh, thank you, Ms. O."

She toned it down the next day. All it took was a gentle nudge. I just couldn't help myself. Saying nothing and letting her go on exposing herself like that would have been the unkind thing to do. And yet her friends, parents, and teachers didn't seem to want to deal with the awkwardness of that conversation. Or they simply didn't care.

I See You

I decided to start an after-school program for these children. I wanted to create a safe place where kids could come and talk to each other in a constructive way. We started with 12 students and ended up with more than 120 in just a few weeks. It became a lifeline for so many kids with nowhere else to go. We did fun stuff like skits, role-play, and exercises to help them in interview situations for jobs and colleges. One time there was a shooting outside in the schoolyard after hours, and we were in our classroom, listening to music and having a good ol' time talking about life. When we stepped outside and saw the local news camera there, my kids asked, "What happened?" A drug deal had turned deadly, and a boy was killed. They were blissfully unaware, because they were safe inside. I shudder to think what would have happened if they'd been hanging around outside.

Pearls and Gems

It's beautiful to see the transformation that can happen in young people when an adult takes the time to notice them. So many of my students have gone on to do great things, including Shakim Compere, Dana's business partner. He's family now. One of my favorite students, Irisa Leverette, was such a quiet little thing when she joined my class. She kept her head down and barely spoke. She wasn't much more than four feet tall and so desperately shy. Unlike my Dana, she didn't walk around with her head held high. But there was just something about her. Her work was brilliant. She had *such intelligence and character. I made it my mission to bring her out of her shell and encourage her academically. Her family didn't have much money, so I made her one of my first scholarship students through our education foundation.*

Irisa did us proud. She went to Kean College (now Kean University), and she is now a history professor at that same school. Her sister was caught up in drugs, so Irisa took custody of her nieces and nephews, including one who is physically and mentally challenged. She adopted three children outright. This little thing turned out to be a pillar of strength. A true queen, she's walking tall today. But when I first met her, it was as if she wanted to hide, and she might have, all her life, if somebody hadn't noticed her. What a waste that would have been! If Irisa had stayed invisible, it would have been the world's loss.

That's why it was so important for me to understand my children as individuals from an early age. I always knew my Dana was extraordinary, and I wanted to understand exactly what it was that made her tick. I wanted her specialness to come out in the safe, nurturing environment of a loving home, so that when she left the nest, all too soon, she could be proud of who she was—proud and unafraid to express it.

At times, I must confess I've resented having to share my daughter with the world. She's wonderful about making time for me and calling regularly, but her life's path takes her across the country and around the world.

I'm not one of these mothers who get to have her children and grandchildren with her at the dinner table every Sunday. I always worry about her and hope that the people who are there to comfort and care for her when she's far away from me truly have her back. But God made me Queen Latifah's mom for a reason. It gives me the opportunity to bring out the potential of thousands more children than I could ever reach in my classroom—through our scholarship foundation, the Urban League, even forums like this book.

I hope and pray that the moments my daughter shares with you will help you stop, look, and appreciate yourself for all the unique and wonderful qualities you bring to this world. I hope you will understand that in many ways, Queen Latifah is just like you. She's suffered the same losses and made many of the same mistakes. And just like my Dana, you will find success and happiness on your own terms when you embrace your authentic self and love and believe in who you are. Keep your checklist by the bathroom mirror. Repeat that list every day until it sinks in and becomes part of your DNA. Even if you don't think anyone really sees you . . . see yourself.

Love,
Mamma O

CHAPTER 5

Fear

Open your eyes 'cause it's time to get live . . .
—LATIFAH, "LONG ASS MOUNTAIN"

Stepping onto that board, I had no idea how small it would be. There wasn't any room for me to take a running leap. The only thing to do was take a deep breath and jump straight in. But as I stared down the thirty-three-foot drop into the swirling turquoise water below, I couldn't breathe. Damn, it was far! My heart flew up into my mouth. The thought flashed through my mind that it might be best if I just backed out gracefully. Maybe, just maybe, I could slink away, and no one would notice.

I was visiting Jamaica with some friends—Shakim and some of our crew from New Jersey, including my boy Timmy, who practically lived at Rick's Café in Negril. Timmy and his sister, a real girl's girl, were up for any adventure: fishing, scuba diving, you name it. So when Timmy and his sister took turns jumping off the cliff like it was nothing, I just had to follow. At first, Shakim was going to join me, but when he got close to the edge and saw what he was in for, he said, "Oh, *hell*, no!"

He begged me not to do it. A long time ago, Shakim made a promise to my mother that he would never let anything happen to me, and he was scared. He didn't want to have to go back home and report to Ms. O that her daughter broke her neck on his watch. But something about that place, with its magical sunset, green hillsides merging into sapphire blue water, dolphins jumping out of the surf—not to mention the free-flowing Jamaican rum cocktails—was daring me to try. I wanted to soak up the full experience, even if that meant getting soaked in the process!

Then the reality of the situation hit me. I tried to gas myself up, but I was terrified. Somebody in the crowd recognized me and yelled out, "Jump! Jump!" Attempting to talk myself into it, I said, "Okay, f— it! Let's do this." (I try to be a lady and keep my language clean, but privately sometimes my foul mouth gets the better of me.) Of course, somebody overheard and started shouting, "F— it! F— it!" Meanwhile, a busload of tourists arrived just in time for my spectacle, and they joined in the chanting: "F— it! F— it! F— it!" The whole crowd was into it. Why, oh why did they have to hear me say that? There was no backing out now.

I jumped feet first, toes pointed down toward the water, my body stiff and braced for the impact. The words "Oh . . . my . . . God" are all I remember thinking before I hit the water, hard. Every cavity was flushed out, but the water was invigorating. I felt giddy, like I could do anything. I swam over to the other side of the cliff, where Timmy and his sister were waiting. They'd already climbed up to another diving platform, five feet higher than the first one, so of course I had to join them. "Okay," we figured, "we can do this again." At this point, there was no other way to get back onto terra firma anyway. When I landed in one piece the second time, the initial thrill had worn off, and I shuddered at the thought of what I'd just put myself through. I finally climbed out of the sea and back to the bar, never to return to Jamaican cliff jumping again! But I was proud of what I'd done. The overwhelming memory of that experience was the exhilaration I felt as I splashed into the water—not the moment of terror I felt before I took the leap.

I guess you could call me a bit of an adrenaline junkie. I enjoy challenging myself and testing the limits of my fear. Because life is so short and so precious, you've got to take a big bite out of it. That means learning, growing, and being open to new things. It means embracing change. There's so much out there I have yet to try, and I'm up for anything.

Fear the Fear

Fear can be crippling. It can paralyze you and cause you to not move or do things that you desire most in your heart. It can hold you back from love or keep you stuck in a pattern or a place where love won't ever find you. You might be afraid that the person you love will leave you or won't love you back. You might be afraid to be your authentic self, believing you'll be rejected if people see who you really are. Fear stops you from feeling the greatest joys in life. Fear kills the real you.

The Jamaican cliff dive moment was one of my more extreme adventures, but I love experiencing the rush that comes from doing something that's way out of my comfort zone. I like to do things that are exciting. There's something about having that little bit of fear and pushing myself to overcome it. It allows me to do so many other things I might not otherwise consider. It makes me feel alive.

Making the movie *Last Holiday* and walking in the shoes of my character, Georgia Byrd, reminded me how important it is to really drop your inhibitions and go for it. Fear was holding this woman back from so much in life. She loved food and she loved to cook, but instead of eating the dishes she created, she'd nuke herself a Lean Cuisine in the microwave because she was afraid of a few extra calories. She had a beautiful voice, but she was so timid that no one in her church choir could hear her sing. She was crazy for a man she worked with, and he was obviously crazy for her, but she was so shy that she couldn't even look him in the eye. Her whole life was stuck inside a wish book in her kitchen drawer, gathering dust.

It's only when she gets the news that she's dying that she really starts to live. That was a powerful message for me, because at the time I was doing nothing but work, work, work, and I wasn't making enough room in my schedule to just enjoy life. It's very easy to get caught up and not notice all the good things that are passing you by. You have to live every day like it's your last.

In the movie, Georgia decides to cash in all her bonds and clear out her savings account and have one last blast before the end came. With nothing left to lose, she goes on a real adventure. She even goes BASE jumping.

That's where I draw the line. No way would I do something that crazy! But I do want to learn how to fly a plane and a helicopter. And I want to skydive. (Okay, maybe it's not much of a line.) My "to do" list of adventures is constantly growing. Each one I check off the list emboldens me to go even further the next time.

I finally learned how to ski after making *Last Holiday*. Around the time we were filming, I learned how to snowboard, but a few months later some crazy Canadian friends of mine were going skiing at Mt. Whistler, British Columbia, and they invited me along. Now this I had to try. As a Jersey girl from the 'hood, I never really saw skiing as a possibility for me. You don't see too many African-Americans in the Winter Olympics. But when I was little, I used to be fascinated by the ski jumping on ABC's *Wide World of Sports*. Watching those athletes soar through the air made me dream about doing the same thing.

Another Big Ass Mountain

We rented a big chalet at the ski resort, and the first day I took a lesson on the bunny slope while my friends skied the more advanced runs. I'd just about mastered the snow plow, and thought I knew enough of the basics to join my friends on the grown-up slopes the next day. One of my girlfriends is a licensed ski instructor, so I figured I'd stick close to her. But I wasn't expecting them to take me all the way to the top of the mountain, and it was a loooong way down to the next chair lift. We're talking miles of trail. I could've killed 'em!

The only way off of this thing was to ski. I tried to follow my ski lesson from the previous day and do my turns, but everything I tried just landed me in a face plant. I must have fallen ten times over the course of a few dozen yards. I was starting to get wet, and cold, and incredibly frustrated. I could see a couple of my friends in the distance talking and imagined the conversation was going something like this:

"Oh, my God, do you think she's gonna lose it?"

"Yeah, she's definitely about to lose it!"

Then my friend the ski instructor shouted, "You can do this, Dana! You can do this!"

Move Your Head Out of the Way

I wasn't so sure. It was like I had some mental block. My body just wouldn't follow through on what my brain was telling it to do. I stood up, looked around me, and realized that the next chair lift was still about a mile and a half down the mountain. I either had to ski down to it or walk in my heavy ski boots. I was still considering my next move when this little kid who couldn't have been more than five years old skied past me without any poles. He was skiing alongside his dad, and the little boy asked him, "Dad, do you think we could make this the last trip down?"

"Sure, son," the dad said. "You did great today."

At first I thought, "What kind of Norman Rockwell painting am I in? Please, Lord, just get me off this mountain!"

Then it occurred to me: If this little kid could do it without any poles, then, dammit, I could do it, too! And all of a sudden I just started skiing. I wasn't thinking about what I was doing, I was just doing it. I just went for it, and all those thoughts in my head disappeared. It was even getting to be kind of fun. I made it down to the chair lift in one piece, cheering, "I did it, I did it!"

Looking back, I realize that I was letting my mind block me. Overthinking is just another form of fear. You almost have to give yourself a mantra and lock into it. As soon as I had that one thought—"I can do this"—I stopped overthinking and it just happened for me. Instinct took over. I started trusting in my body to get me down the mountain. Something just clicked inside me. I don't know how. It was that one moment, looking at that child, and I was thanking God for it.

I love skiing now. I was always one of these

people who went to hot places for vacations, and now I enjoy going to the mountains just as much. Feeling the crisp air on my face, that sensation of falling as you slice through the snow on a pair of skis, swimming outside in the cold and staying warm in a pool that's hot and steamy . . . I faced a challenge and found even more in life that gives me joy. It's just one of many things that have broadened my life. Opening your world to different things, whether it's art, culture, music, food, even different kinds of people, is so much more interesting than just doing the same thing over and over.

There's another benefit to challenging yourself and testing the next limit of your fear. When you do, and you make that leap of faith in yourself and your God, everything somehow falls into place and becomes easier. Then you ask yourself, "What was holding me back? What was all the fuss about?" Pushing past the scary stuff is the only way to move yourself forward in life.

I was lucky to have a dad and a big brother who never doubted my ability to keep up with them, whatever the adventure. Winki was always encouraging me, waking me up early to include me in whatever trouble he could concoct for us. And when it came to sports, fishing, or camping, Dad never excluded me from the fun. He taught both my brother and me how to shoot. He'd take us to the firing range or into the woods to fire at tin cans, and I got to be pretty good at it.

I remember one time, when Winki was twenty-one and he'd just been made Newark's youngest police officer on the force, we decided to go to the firing range. I had my Glock 17 handgun, and he'd just been issued a shiny new SIG P229 Smith & Wesson revolver, and we were ready to shoot some stuff up! I knew we were going to get competitive, and I figured I probably didn't have a chance with all the police training and target practice Winki'd had. But when we got to the range, put on our headsets, and settled into our booths, I just went for it. While Winki was doing everything perfectly, taking his time and steadying himself between shots, I fired round after round, "Pow, pow, pow!" cursing out the target like it was a real assailant. There was no technique to my shooting, just raw instinct and emotion. When we pulled back our sheets of paper, I couldn't believe it. I got *way* more bull's-eyes than my brother. It was one of the few times I actually beat him! And it was another lesson that sometimes it's best to trust your gut.

When You Think, You Stink

My point is that when you throw your heart and soul into something without overanalyzing it, you can excel. You're at your best when you're focused on the task and fully absorbed in what you are doing, not even considering whether or not you are performing the task to perfection.

Of course, you have to have a little bit of fear. I'm not saying you should be reckless. But fear shouldn't be the front-running emotion. It's good to have that smidgen of nervousness that makes you aware of what's going on around you. But be bold and give way to your instincts.

I was recently in a Ford Mustang campaign where I got to ride around a track with NASCAR champion Colin Braun. (As a kid, I used to love watching NASCAR on TV, but, as with skiing, I never dreamed a little black girl from New Jersey would have an opportunity like that. You don't see too many black folks behind those wheels.) First Colin drove me around the circuit, really fast. Then he got out of the driver's seat and let me take over the wheel. I got the car to a buck thirty on this small track, flying through corners. It was amazing. I wasn't scared, but I had just enough fear to create an awareness. I was energized. That kind of fear makes everything around you clearer. It heightens your senses and puts you in tune with your body, your hand placement, what your mind is doing. It's almost like you are stepping outside of yourself and seeing everything that is going on, while still feeling the speed and every little bump and curve of the track.

When I ride my motorbike, it's a similar feeling, except that there's nothing between you and the road. There's no metal protecting you, no seat belts, no bumpers. It's just you and God. Your eyes have to be really focused. You have to see what's coming up in front of you. You have to be aware of some pothole in the ground in front of you or a car that's braking three cars ahead of the one in front of you. You're driving the whole road, not just your bike and the vehicle up ahead. You're taking it all in so you can keep yourself safe.

An experienced rider knows how to balance speed with heightened awareness. But when I first started riding, there were times when I had no idea how fast I was going.

I was about twenty-one when one of my friends brought home a picture of a motorcycle I just had to have. When Shakim saw my bike, he had to have one, too. We tended to do things together. The problem was, neither of us knew how to ride. Shakim's brother Paul was a biker, so he taught us in the parking lot of his building, and I slowly started to get the feel of it. My brother was a real motorcycle fan, and I knew I couldn't have this fine ride without giving him one, so a few months later we all chipped in and bought the same model bike for Winki on his twenty-fourth birthday. Pretty soon, a crew of one hundred of us would start riding around together. But my brother was the best. He drove the fastest—too fast sometimes. That was Winki. Nothing was half speed. And he loved that bike like nothing else.

Drop the Hammer!

We called ourselves "the Redliners" because we always hit speeds up in the red line of the speedometer. My brother would say, "Come on, Dana, let's tear it up today!" And we'd hit the throttle and fly. I still wasn't that experienced a rider, but I liked to stay at the back of the front pack, where most of my friends were riding. Two brothers I knew from grammar school, Phil and Leon, were serious riders, and they were tearing up the road, but there was no way I was going to be separated from them, so I dropped the hammer, going faster and faster, until I looked at the needle and realized I was going 155 miles! I thought, "Whoa! What the heck just took over me?" I slowed back down to my own pace. As much as I like going fast, for me that kind of speed was just crazy.

But when my brother and I rode together, we were perfectly in sync. Around the time we got the bikes, I'd just bought my mother a house that we could all live in: I would get the top floor, my mother the middle floor, and Winki would be in the basement. I was on the road a lot, touring for my second album, and I missed my mother and brother. We were all living in separate apartments, and on the night or two I got to be home, I didn't always have the time to drive out and see them both. This was my way of keeping my family close.

I found a contemporary house in a nice, quiet suburban neighborhood, but it was brand new and still raw. We needed flooring, hardware, lighting, plumbing, everything. Winki knew a thing or two about hardware, so whenever we had free time together, we'd ride out to Manhattan's Chinatown and look at all the lighting and plumbing fixture shops, grab something to eat, then gun it fast and hard on the way back home to New Jersey. They were some of the happiest times in my life.

Standing Alone

Redlining down a highway, flying down a mountain, diving out of a plane—these are scary things. But some of the scariest moments in life have nothing to do with jumping off a cliff. They're about facing down your demons or having the moral courage to walk away when you know something's not right.

When I was a child, my scariest times were when I felt I had to break away from the pack. Mom and Dad warned me there would be times when I would have to stand alone or fight back, and I dreaded those moments. I stood firm, but inside I was trembling. Sometimes I had to face down a bully or risk being unpopular with the cool crowd when they were talking about doing drugs or hanging out in a bad neighborhood late at night.

I didn't always make the right choices. But my bad decisions were more out of an overwhelming curiosity than fear of what other people thought of me. I was very young when I'd sneak off to New York City with my brother or a crew of friends. I was barely into my teens when I started experimenting with drugs and sex. But that ability to stand alone was what stopped me from taking it so far down the line that I couldn't come back without some permanent damage. I would try something once, realize it would be all too easy to get addicted, and never go there again, despite what all my so-called friends were trying to get me into. When I realized I was taking something too far, I didn't have a problem with walking away, despite what everyone else was doing. I was more afraid of disappointing my parents and letting myself down than losing favor with the cool kids.

Flat on My Face

Fear of failure was another thing I had to overcome. I was a competitive kid, and I expected to be good at whatever I put my hand to, but you can't ace everything. When I was eight, I tried out for the neighborhood kickball team without ever having played before. I just thought I could do it. I went out there and gave it my all. Somebody kicked the ball at me, and it came so fast that I thought I would catch it, but it bounced right off my stomach and I didn't make the catch. I got cut from the tryouts that day, and I'd never felt more dejected. The walk home wasn't very long, but it seemed like forever. I came home crying. My mom made dinner for me, gave me a hug, and told me that she loved me and she was proud of me for trying and doing my best. She told me it was going to be okay, and she was right. Rejection didn't break me. It just made me that much more determined to succeed. Learning this lesson so young was a blessing, because it's something you can apply at any stage of your life. You can't excel at anything in life without a few failures under your belt. Embrace them, because they will make you bold.

When you are consumed by a fear of failure, it's almost a foregone conclusion. I learned that lesson as a junior in high school when I took a public speaking class. I had to learn a section of Martin Luther King's "I Have a Dream" speech. I didn't study it as much as I could have, and I didn't sleep well the night before, because I was so worried I'd bomb. The next day we had to go up against another school, and I had to get up in front of this class full of unfamiliar faces and a few I did know from the neighborhood. Of course, I butchered my speech. I tried to be passionate about it, but I went completely blank at times. I got through it, but I missed key lines. My palms were sweating, my throat was dry, and I stumbled over the words. I was terrified I was going to blow it, which I proceeded to do when I got up there. But something else happened. *I survived*. No matter how bad you think it is, it really isn't. You live through it and you learn from it.

I did much better the next time. Taking that class and facing those fears allowed me to be able to get up in front of an audience full of people and host the American Music Awards or host a talk show in front of a live audience every day for two seasons, thinking on my feet and controlling the flow of the conversation. It allows me to speak in a roomful of people and be unafraid to go into meetings to pitch an idea I believe in. I can go into a room, face high-powered executives, producers, or financiers who can make it happen, and not be the least bit intimidated. Without that early experience of seriously flubbing my lines and living through it, I never would have had the confidence I have today. Failure is not the end of the world, but never even trying is a travesty.

In my sophomore year, when I switched to Irvington High School where my mother taught, I set the bar even higher for myself. That year they had a big talent show, and even though I didn't know a lot of people at the school, I really wanted to enter my name and be a part of it. But just walking out onto that stage, I was so nervous that my hands were shaking. I started singing "If Only for One Night" by Luther Vandross, and the more I continued to sing, the more comfortable I felt. I glanced down at the audience and saw something in one person's eyes and something in another person's eyes—it was a look that said, "Wow, she can sing!" That was the spark I needed to start owning that song. I lost myself in it, and my fears melted away. I nailed it and got an amazing response from the crowd.

That moment brought me several steps closer to my music career. I started performing with friends, doing beat box in the girls' restroom at school, rhyming and making beats on the bathroom stall door. I made friends with other kids from around the way who shared my passion, like my boy DJ Mark and Shakim. Once I discovered hip-hop, there was no turning back.

Facing your fear is the one true path to your future—your destiny. Sometimes we fear the things we desire the most, because we are so terrified we'll mess them up. But think of what you'd be missing out on if you didn't even try.

Say It Loud

I have a close friend who has the most brilliant ideas. He comes up with amazing concepts like it's nothing. He's so creative about all kinds of things, whether it's a merchandising scheme or something related to a film or music project. This guy is a magnificent master planner, and he's opened up my mind to endless possibilities. But he's terrible in meetings. Every time we get in a room with the money people to make it happen, he chokes up. He doesn't say a word, and he freaks. We would literally be sitting in a conference room with his idea—an idea I wanted him to present himself—and he couldn't speak, so I had to do it for him.

Imagine how far my friend could go, and what he could become, if he would just open his mouth and say what he felt and thought. He's paralyzed by fear, and it makes me sad. I tried to tell him, "This is your idea, you've got to go in and sell it." This was his baby, but he couldn't raise it, or feed it, or do anything with the baby he gave birth to because he couldn't, or wouldn't, bring himself to speak.

I'm glad I bombed more than once because I knew what it was like to fail, and I knew I could survive it, dust myself off, and get better the next time. That feeling of falling flat on your face is tough to deal with. It's uncomfortable. It makes you feel raw, exposed, humiliated. But you'll live through it and be better with the knowledge you gained from your mistakes. Even if you are feeling uncertain, you have to front a little bit. Try acting like you've got the courage and confidence, even if you're nervous, so you can trick yourself into believing it. Make it a mantra. Say those affirmations out loud. When you wake up and tell yourself today is going to be a good day, you put that in your mind. You put the energy out there.

Of course, it's natural to have a little bit of fear.

I'm not gonna lie to you—there are a lot of situations that make me nervous. When I'm preparing for a new movie role and I'm about to share the screen with Oscar-winning actors like Denzel Washington or Holly Hunter, or any other great actor who's been doing it far longer than I have, I get intimidated. But it's a healthy kind of fear, because it makes you want to do a great job. It doesn't make me not want to act, it just makes me more aware of what I'm doing.

I had to face some fear recently when I was filming *Just Wright*. My character has a love scene with the character played by Common, and it's the most intimate I've ever had to be on camera. I did a kissing scene before in *Beauty Shop*. But despite the fact that I got to kiss Djimon Hounsou, a really hot guy, doing it on film feels awkward. It's not like I ever saw myself kissing before. I know what it feels like. I know I'm good at it, and I know I feel sexy when I'm kissing, but I never had to worry about whether or not a camera angle is making me look crazy while I'm doing it.

Now multiply that anxiety by a factor of a hundred. I'd heard other actors talk about doing love scenes and how embarrassing it can be with all those people in the room—the director, the cameraman, the lighting guys, the grips. I knew I'd have to be vulnerable and expose some sides of myself, both emotionally and physically. I had to put all of this private stuff on-screen, with no idea how I looked. But you know something? I got through it, and the end product was as tasteful as I'd hoped it would be. Despite my jitters, I had to get into that moment and that character and push through my inhibitions. It's the only way you can grow as an actor and a human being.

I was even more intimidated when I had to do a scene with a group of women who were not professional actors. These were real women who were HIV-positive, playing themselves in a scene for an HBO movie called *Life Support*. It was based on the true story of writer/director Nelson George's sister Ana, a wife and mother who overcame her addiction to crack to become a peer counselor for an AIDS outreach program in Brooklyn. Looking at the real Ana walking down Flatbush Avenue was almost like looking at a mirror image of myself, we're so similar. We're both Pisces. We're both headstrong. We're both curious about life in ways that could get us into trouble.

I grew up around women like Ana, in the same streets at around the same time, and I did some of the same things. I felt like I could really relate to the characters, to the situations, to a family disrupted by drug addiction. I could relate to all of that just in my own family. I could relate to Ana's sense of wanting to get out there and see what life had to offer, although we took dramatically different turns. I could relate to her desire for redemption as well, for wanting the second chance to try to repair those relationships. I've had the same thoughts. I've said to myself, "Okay, I messed up, but I'm back on track and I really want to get things back to where they were."

Dig Deep

In the group session scene, I play Ana, opening up about her guilt and her frustration as she tries to reconnect with the daughter she left in the care of her mother when she was still addicted to crack. I wanted to be respectful of the other women in the room. They had all kinds of stories, yet they were walking through life, facing this disease. I had to be humble about it, and respectful, because these women do amazing things in the name of HIV prevention and outreach every day. I didn't want this to be a movie that was taking advantage of other people's stories. They were real women who faced many of the same situations I lived through. I had to make it real, so I dug deep into my past, from the time I was just Dana, a teenager experimenting and trying to figure out who I was. Those were times when I took chances I probably shouldn't have taken. I took myself back to those places where things occurred in my life I'm not proud of; where I did things that made me feel dirty and ashamed. So what came across on the screen was pure, raw emotion. I was living through the pain again. It was like opening up a vein. And I'd do it all over again.

Making that movie was life-affirming in so many ways. I was so passionate about the subject that the time between reading the script and shooting the first scene was a month—that's unheard of! I knew it would be a tough film to make, but it was a story that had to be told. It made me realize how fortunate I was. While we were shooting, I was walking down some of those streets thinking, "My God, I could still be here. I could have contracted HIV." It made me aware of how serious the issue still is, especially for young black women. I was one of the lucky ones. I made it out of those situations I was putting myself in when I was fifteen, sixteen, and seventeen years old. I had a newfound respect for the courage of these women who weren't so fortunate; who'd lived through the worst but had the strength of character to keep moving forward, living their lives and helping others.

Brave Heart

Being fearless is about so much more than the dare-devil stunts I tend to enjoy. My mother is the most courageous person I know, but she wouldn't be caught dead on a motorcycle. As a matter of fact, when I was just a baby, a motorbike accident almost killed her. She was riding on the back of my father's bike when someone swerved into them. The doctors gave her some experimental drug to stop the pain from her injuries, and it almost shut her body down. So no, my mother won't necessarily be joining me on my first skydive. But every day she teaches me what it means to have the heart of a lioness.

When my mother was an art teacher at Irvington High School, she devoted herself to those kids. The more troubled the students, the more love she gave them. Over the years, she could see what was happening to the middle-class community where the school was based. Drugs were a major problem. More students were dealing and using, and so were their parents. More kids were coming out of broken homes and bringing that anger into the classroom. Gang violence would erupt in the schoolyard on a regular basis. Knifings and shootings were commonplace.

Many times, I begged my mother to quit because I could see it was taking a physical toll. She didn't need the work. I could afford to retire her. But instead she took on more classes and started a weekly after-school program to help some of the kids who were having personal problems turn their lives around. Ms. O cared for those kids so much, she routinely put herself in harm's way without any consideration for her own safety. One time, a seventeen-year-old girl twice her size was about to beat in the head of another girl for stealing her boyfriend. This young lady was crazed, but my mother was determined to stop her from getting herself expelled from school, so she grabbed on to her legs and held on for dear life. The girl dragged her for a few yards down the hall, but my mother slowed her down just enough to allow the other girl to escape. The next morning, the young lady was plenty contrite about what she did to my mother.

"Oh, Ms. O, I'm so sorry I dragged you like that!" she said. "Are you okay?"

Another time, my mother walked into a classroom in the middle of a lover's spat: A boy the size of a line-backer was giving his girlfriend a beat-down. He had a chair raised and was ready to smash it over his girl-friend's head, but my mother placed herself between them. She stopped the fight. When I heard about what happened, I was horrified.

"Ma!" I said. "Weren't you worried something was gonna happen to you?"

"Well, Dana," she said, "I'm still here."

This quiet, gentle lady moves through her world unafraid because of her abiding love for her students. She's more concerned about the harm they might do to themselves than to her. "They're just babies," my mother says. "This is what God put me here to do. With the right amount of attention and love, they still have a chance in life. They can change."

My mother's love, and her unwavering faith in God, trumps fear every time.

CHAPTER 6

Loss

You don't ever get over something like this.
You get through it.
—Elaine Owens

Your brother had an accident on his motorcycle."

I heard the words, but my brain couldn't process them. Until that moment, it was just another ordinary day, like any other on an early spring afternoon in New Jersey. The sun was shining, the crocuses were blooming, and the air had that new-life smell to it. After a grueling schedule of touring in Europe for my second album, I finally had some time to chill out with my friends and family, and for the past several days I'd been doing just that. I was thrilled to be home, hanging out with my homies, seeing my mom, catching up with my brother, and riding around with our Redliner bike crew. I was enjoying all the regular stuff I always did before my music career blew up. In fact, I'd just finished helping a friend move his couch to a new apartment in Jersey City. After hauling that thing up three flights of stairs, a bunch of us had just collapsed on the floor and cracked open a beer when I got the 911 page from my brother's boy Ramsey.

"Is it . . . is it bad?" I asked him, already guessing the answer from the tone in his voice.

"I think so," he said, almost in a whisper.

My heart sank, and I felt the blood rush from my head. I was dizzy and confused. I couldn't think. I couldn't move. I just dropped the phone to my side and tried to let the reality of the situation sink in. But the more it did, the more unreal it felt.

The rest of the story unfolded like some sickening nightmare. I don't even know how it happened, but the next thing I remember was Shakim bundling me into his car. We flew down the highway to University Hospital in Newark, where they'd taken my brother. Shakim was driving fast, but it felt like we were in slow motion. When we approached a red light, I screamed at him to gun it. Stopping was out of the question. I wanted nothing more than to get to that hospital. I *had* to see my brother.

Faster, Shakim!

As we were driving along, the blue skies turned gray, then black, and it started to pour. This storm just came out of nowhere. That's when I knew how bad it was. I could feel it. Right before something horrible like that happens, you get this knowledge, this little voice inside you letting you know that whatever it is, something's about to take place and you'd better brace yourself. It could be that hunch you get the moment before your car gets into an accident or a nagging fear when you're out too late on a deserted street in the wrong kind of neighborhood. It's like God is trying to give you a heads-up. Whether or not you're ready to hear it, He's just letting you know. He's preparing you for what is about to go down.

I wasn't prepared, but I already knew. Winki and I had this connection—a bond. We were both Pisces— two fish swimming up the stream together. He was two years older than me, and he was my hero. We always knew what the other was thinking. It was like we were twins. It was the type of spiritual kinship that only the tightest of siblings can share. But something told me our tie had been severed.

As we drove into the darkness with the rain whipping into the windshield, we could barely see the road in front of us, but I didn't care. *"Faster, Shakim! Go! Go!"* As we pulled up to the emergency entrance, I recognized the motorcycle in the back of a tow truck—the Kawasaki Ninja ZX7 we'd bought him for his birthday. It was mangled and smashed and looked as if it would have been impossible to escape serious injury unless he'd somehow managed to jump off it before it crashed. I started pleading and bargaining with God: "Please, Lord. Please make it all right! I'll do anything. If nothing else, just this once!"

The car was still moving when I opened the door and ran out. As soon as I got inside, I saw my brother's crew.

"Where is he? Where's my brother? Is he okay?"

They didn't speak. They didn't have to. I could see it in their faces.

My mom was there in the waiting room, and her eyes were wet from tears. I collapsed into her arms, crying, hoping, and praying. She was eerily calm. She told me in a soft, steady cadence exactly what happened.

"Dana, Winki's been hit and his bike went under the car. Now all we can do is wait."

So we waited. And waited some more. The anticipation was unbearable, but we didn't really want that pain to end, because there was still hope. Then the doctor came into the room. She was still in her scrubs, and she looked haggard and strained. She pulled off her surgical gloves, lowered her mask, and peered down at my mother and me as we sat, clinging together and trembling on the hard waiting room chairs. Then she spoke.

"I'm sorry. He's gone."

There was a second of stunned silence. Then it came out.

"No, he is *not!*" I yelled. "*No!* You ain't telling me this crap! You have to do something! Get back in there and help my brother! Get back in there!"

Circuit Overload

I was out of my mind. The tears were flowing so fast, I couldn't see. I was screaming and yelling, but the doctors kept their cool. I guess they've seen this type of thing before. They told us they took extraordinary measures to save my brother. They cracked open his chest and used twice as much blood as they normally would on a patient in his condition, because he was a cop.

We were crying and shaking and trying to make it make sense. But that's the thing with death. It's non-negotiable. Nothing and nobody can do anything to change it. And even though you know it, you don't accept it. But my brother was gone, and he wasn't coming back.

That was without a doubt the worst moment of my life. It was life-stopping in every sense. I literally stopped living. It was like when an electric circuit gets a surge of power and it just can't deal, so it shuts down. Right then and there, a part of me died along with my brother. The only thing is, after all these years, I still feel the pain. Even now, eighteen years later, I can't talk or write about Winki's passing without tearing up. A line in "Over the Mountain," a song I wrote on my last album, *Persona*, sums it up best: "Wish I could share it all with Wink, and I can still see his face every time I blink."

That kind of loss is something you never get over. It leaves a void that stays with you for the rest of your life. You cope and you deal and you learn to move on. But for me, after that night, my life wasn't the same. And I know deep down in my heart it never will be.

I know I'm not alone in this. Many of you have suffered this same kind of pain. Everyone goes through loss in life. No one is exempt from it. It doesn't matter if you're rich or famous or beautiful or not. Life will come down hard on you, and you've got to get back up one way or another. You hit a fork in the road and you can choose either to deal or to self-destruct. For me, that turning point was my brother's death. You get through it, but not past it. Because you don't stop loving that person. But you have to keep going. The key is to go in the right direction.

It took me a long minute to decide. Losing someone so young, with his whole future ahead of him, is unfathomable. My heart breaks for the thousands of family members who've lost sons, daughters, brothers, sisters, fathers, mothers, wives, and husbands in Iraq and Afghanistan. How do you ever make sense of a loss like that? I understand exactly what Janet Jackson is going through now. She lost her big brother, too. A few months after his death, she was on an interview with *20/20*, and she said it all: "I guess you have to accept what is. But it's just so . . . *hard.*"

The suddenness of a tragedy like this is cruel. You don't even get to say good-bye. Someone who is a huge part of your life is ripped away from you, with no warning. You also know it won't be the last time you have to go through losing someone. The longer we're here on this earth, the more people we love get taken away from us, and there ain't a damn thing we can do about it. The only thing we can control is whether we start living again, or not. For months, and months, and months, I chose not.

Cue the Rain

I was numb. Angry. Guilty. I had every kind of nega-
tive emotion. I blamed God. I blamed myself. That
bike I gave Winki for his birthday, the one that gave
him so much joy to ride, took his life. I'd lost my rock.
My protector. My anchor. The one who made me
laugh and believed I could do anything. It was a grief
that goes so deep, you can't find the bottom. It's
something you just don't understand until you've
been through it. You swing between disbelief, denial,
and uncontrollable sadness. I'd wake up crying and fill
my day playing basketball until I was ready to drop,
then drink until I fell asleep. I'd wake up the next
morning in tears, because nothing I could do would
block out the reality that was waiting for me. I stopped
working. I dumped my boyfriend. I wanted to love
him. I even wanted to get married. But the emotions
kept shutting off. There was no point.

A few years before Winki died, when I was just
starting to gain some traction on my music career
and good things were coming our way, I wondered
if there'd be some ultimate, cosmic price to pay for
the success I craved. I don't know if superstitious is
the word, but too much of the good life made me
nervous. Maybe it dates back to my childhood,
when I thought we had the perfect family and my

parents' decision to separate seemed to come out of nowhere. Ever since then, I didn't quite trust happiness. Deep down, in the recesses of my mind, I was afraid fame and fortune's price would be the loss of someone dear to me, like my mother, my father, or my brother.

So when I did lose Winki, I guess I resented my success. I love and appreciate all that I have now. But even today, if you ask me or my mother if we'd trade places with our lives as they are now for what they were back when we had no money and were living in the projects, we'd do it in a heartbeat if it meant getting Winki back. And the irony is, my career had reached a high point at the time of my brother's accident. Right before Winki died, I was on top of the world with a hit album and a top ten single. I was nominated for a Grammy. I'd just had a ball doing a part in Spike Lee's *Jungle Fever*. And then my brother passed, and I stopped caring. When I actually won the Grammy, it kinda made me smile, but only for a second. There was too much sadness for me to be in the moment and really enjoy it. Nothing seemed to matter anymore. Shakim begged me to get back into the studio. We had another album due, but I wasn't interested.

This whole time, I didn't realize how terrified my mother was for me. I was too locked in my own grief to see how it was affecting the people around me. There was a moment where my mom suddenly stopped crying in the hospital. It was because she realized she had to be strong for me. The hurt she was feeling was profound. She'd lost her baby boy, her firstborn. But she was scared she was about to lose another child. She was afraid I'd lose myself in the darkness of my grief and never find my way back.

My dad took it hard, too. He kept saying, "They took my chicken." That was his nickname for Wink because he kept him under his wing. But he'd lost a few precious years with his baby boy. Dad had some problems with trauma from the Vietnam War and being an undercover cop that led him to substance abuse, and for a few years he wasn't as accessible to us as he wanted to be. He lost Wink just as they were getting close again. His heart burst with pride when his beloved son followed in his footsteps and joined the police force. Then Wink was taken away from us all. It made my father really focus on all his children, doing everything he could to make up for the time he lost with all of us.

But I couldn't focus on anyone but Winki. I was stuck in a long moment of grief and despair. I clawed my way out of it slowly. At first, I got through the endless days by going to Winki's grave and talking to him. Somehow it brought me peace. But the real healing started when I got back on my motorbike. I wasn't scared to ride, exactly. A motorbike—or at least the vulnerability of being on a motorbike—was what killed my brother, and somehow it felt like a betrayal to do that thing we enjoyed so much together, because that was the very thing that took him away from me and my family.

Back on the Bike

But my brother's spirit was asking me to ride, and live, for his sake, and he's been on the bike with me ever since. That freedom—the feeling of the wind on your face and the body, the sound of the engine, its roaring power—was what gave my brother and me such joy during his short time on this earth. I still wear the key to Winki's bike on a gold chain around my neck when I'm feeling sad. And when I ride, I ride for both of us. When I'm hugging those roads, whether I'm driving the coastal highways of California or tearing up the New Jersey interstates, it's almost spiritual. I'm in control of the bike and holding its handlebars, but I'm not in control, because at a certain speed it's just me and God. There are no cell phones, no distractions, just me and the elements. I feel excitement, joy, and oneness with the universe. When I'm on that bike, I'm talking to Winki. And I'm talking to God. I'm saying, "Okay, Lord, take care of me now. I'm in Your hands."

Shakim and my mother were so relieved to see me back on my bike, because they knew it also meant that I had decided to come back to life. Then I actually started to work again. It wasn't so much that I cared about getting another hit record. I just needed an outlet to express what I was going through. I needed my music to heal. I started writing songs for my album *Black Reign*, including a tribute to my brother called "Winki's Theme." I stayed up all night writing that joint. I was living in the house I'd bought for me and my mother and brother to all live in together (not that the three of us got the chance). Mom was asleep in her room upstairs, but at five a.m., I just had to wake her up. I wanted to share what I'd created with the one person who would understand every word in that song the way I did. She heard it, smiling, crying, and nodding her head to the music all at the same time. It was a message of pure love for my brother, and we both knew that he'd be rocking to it all the way up in heaven. Mom later said the album title perfectly summed up my life in that moment: It was a black period, but one over which I would ultimately reign. The queen inside me was alive again.

Why Me, Lord? Why Me?

It's funny how art imitates life, life imitates art. Years later I made *Last Holiday*, a movie that addresses, in a lighthearted way, the crossroads where we have a choice between living full out and giving up on life altogether. (I mention this film a lot because it made a huge impression on me.) My character, Georgia Byrd, gets the news that she has weeks to live. After a miserable night alone at home, polishing off a bottle of wine, she turns up in church for her gospel choir recital. When they start to sing, this repressed, wound-up little thing who's too shy to belt out a song, starts talking out loud, in full voice, to her God. "Why me, O Lord, why me!" she says over and over and over again. The church ladies love it. They think Georgia is speaking in tongues, and they join in. But Georgia really means it. What the . . . ? God, why are You doing this to me? What did I do to deserve this? She's mad as hell at Him, and she wants answers.

Georgia Byrd was inspired, or you could say she was forced, to just go live. She had to make a decision to either lie down and die right there or pick up and live all of the dreams and desires that she's had all this time but held back on for one reason or another, mostly fear and worry. Her character inspired me to live better.

You don't realize sometimes when you play these roles that they're going to impact your life the way they do. Living in Georgia Byrd's life for a few months made me realize how important life is, how short time is, how important it is to follow your dreams and your goals.

Everybody at some point has that "why" moment: "Why me?" "Why us?" "Why my mom?" "Why my dad?" "Why him and not me?" When my brother died, I don't even know if it was just a "why me?" But it was surely a big old "why." Now, instead of thinking, "Why me?" I realize, "Why *not* me?" "Why anybody?"

But I was able to come through it and kind of open myself up to the divine design of it all. The loss of someone I love was not something that I liked or expected. Bad things happen in life, but it's hard to see beyond our own pain. I didn't want to be alone with my thoughts. I didn't want to process my grief. I'd stay out late and party until I couldn't stay awake anymore and then just sleep as long as I could. But all that stuff just covers it up for a minute. At some point, you have to get back into the race. I know that's what those who pass would want for us. If I'd continued down that path and failed to live my best life, I'd have dishonored my brother's memory. I couldn't stand the thought of disappointing Winki.

There but for the Grace of God Do I Go . . .

People would say to me, "Sorry about your brother, can I have your autograph?" And I would think, "You don't care about me, you don't care about my brother, all you care about is your stupid autograph. For what? To prove to your friends you met a celebrity?" It seemed so dumb and shallow. I'd be thinking, "I'm in pain and you know it—but you don't care about Queen Latifah, she's not a human to you." It really bummed me out, but as I got more and more in touch with my spiritual side, I came to understand how these folks don't mean anything by it. They're just people. They just don't understand. It's like when Jesus said: "Forgive them, for they know not what they do." If Jesus could do it while he was being persecuted, who am I not to be able to do it when people are paying me compliments!

So I came to realize that this was a part of my test. Instead of expecting everyone to feel my pain, I had to turn it around and see how they have *their* own lives and problems they were coping with, and my celebrity just represents an escape from those difficult times. Maybe it was something I sang that made them feel good. Maybe it was something I said that made them laugh. They felt a connection to that, so they feel a connection to me. I can't ever forget that's an honor. It's an honor to be someone who can make others happy. That's all they wanted. I came to appreciate it wasn't all just about *my* pain. Pain is all around.

There's an Angel Watching over Me . . .

Therapy helped. I learned there's a process that everyone goes through when they grieve, and it takes longer than you think. But what ultimately got me through it was my faith in God, even though I blamed Him for doing this to me in the first place. I really believe that God had His hands on me the whole time, and my family as well. We came through it when we didn't think we could. All of this pain taught me something. Somehow, through the fog, I remember one particular thought was planted in my brain—I think by God, but maybe it was Winki: "Don't let it all go." Don't let everything go, because you're going to make it through this. God gives you some skills, and it's your responsibility to use them. It's a gift, and you don't turn down gifts and you don't not appreciate them. That's part of who you are. It's the reason we're all here.

I won't lie—I know I've been blessed. I've been lucky. Sure, I worked hard, but I'm not so big not to know I couldn't do it without help—from family, friends, and God. And along with all that good, there's got to be some bad. That's life on this earth. We ain't in heaven yet! And until it's our time, we've got work to do.

I now know my brother is where he was supposed to be, and so am I. We'll all be together eventually. Winki's job on earth was done. He made peace with God before he went. He was proud and happy. He was about to settle down and marry the love of his life. He was a respected member of the police force. He was loved by friends too numerous to count. He was adored by his mom and baby sister. His dad was beyond proud of him. He was a good man who lived life full out, and in doing so, he set an example for us all. He accomplished what God wanted him to do. God has a plan for all of us.

Winki was a cop. Sometimes I think maybe he went in this way so he wouldn't go in a worse way. Maybe something bad out there didn't happen to him, something that would have been worse for all of us. I don't know. I always leave myself open to the possibility that things happen for a reason, and I don't always understand that reason, but it's something I have to accept.

Life has a way of reminding you that you're not immortal and that tragedy can strike any one of us, anytime. That's why you need to have faith. I'm not saying you necessarily have to believe in God. You don't have to be Christian, Muslim, Hindu, or Jewish. But you need to open yourself up to an idea that's bigger than you are. It could be compassion or a faith in the basic goodness of mankind. Even just a sense of the spiritual, or a trust that there are benign forces in the universe that we don't necessarily understand, will give us the strength to take those steps toward living our best life.

When we're going through some crisis, God is whispering to us the whole time. He's not shouting, "Hey, yo, listen up!" By the time you get that message loud and clear, He's already tried to tell you a few times. He gave you plenty of signs. You just weren't paying attention.

About five years ago, I was running myself ragged and enjoying a few too many drinks at night. It tends to happen when I'm busy and I don't take the time to check in with myself or communicate what I need to the people around me. I have a strong constitution, and that might not be such a good thing, because I don't always know when to slow down. It served me well at the beginning of my career when much of our business was conducted in the nightclub, but it's not how I should be living my life as a grown woman. It's not good for me. There were times when I'd drink so much, I would black out the next morning.

One night I was out at a club in L.A. with my assistant, and it was her turn to drink and have fun, so I agreed to be the designated driver. I figured one drink would be okay, but then one drink led to two and possibly three. I wasn't impaired, but it was just one of those nights when everything goes wrong. It was my time of the month—a sign that I should have probably just stayed home. It was also a full moon, and there's always something about a full moon that messes with you.

A cop pulled me over, not because I was over the speed limit or doing anything wrong, but because someone earlier that night had gone on a shooting spree in the area, and they were driving a vehicle similar to mine. Well, that did it. The cops could smell a little alcohol on my breath, and they made me take all the sobriety tests. They'd just changed the acceptable alcohol limits in the state of California from 1.0 to 0.8, and of course, the way my evening was going, I was just over, at 0.9. They took me to the station, where I was questioned by Officer Laffer. Laffer! I thought, "You've got to be kidding me." It was like God was laughing at me!

I had to pay a fine and take a remedial driving course, and they recommended I attend an AA meeting. I was not happy. When I went to the driving class, I told the instructor how unfair it was. I wasn't even driving impaired. But he said something that really changed my perspective.

"Think about how many times you drove home at night and you *were* driving impaired."

He was right. There probably were a few times. There were moments I felt the angels must have been guiding me home safely, because I really shouldn't have been behind the wheel.

Famous people with money can lawyer up and get charges dropped easily. I could have gotten out of that DUI. But because of what that instructor told me, I decided to suck it up and deal with the consequences. I even went to the AA meeting. I didn't have to, but I wanted to check in with myself. I wanted to know, "Am I okay?"

At the meeting, everyone introduced themselves and did what they call "sharing." One guy said, "I'm frustrated because I had a lot of things to do at work today, and I didn't get to all of it." Another man shared that he was having problems communicating with his teenage daughter. A woman shared that she was six months sober.

It was small stuff. But by being in that meeting and opening up about all those little things, like not getting through a task list, these people were saving themselves from the temptation of going to a bar after work. It taught me that I can't let my own frustra-

tions pile up like that. I had to do a better job of communicating how I really felt.

I asked the leader of that session how you know if
you're really an alcoholic. He gave me a quiz, and I
learned that I am not. I can go without a drink. I can
stop at a certain point if I choose to. But I was definitely borderline. And with a history of alcoholism in
my family (some aunts and uncles were big drinkers),
I needed to be careful. It was just the wake-up call I
needed.

That whole incident was God's little way of
saying, "Take it easy, Dana." He gave me a little spank
in the form of a DUI charge, just to let me know. I
wasn't listening to Him before, so He had to shout in
my ear this time. It wasn't the first situation like this
I found myself in, but you can bet it was the last.

Having faith has gotten me through so much in
life. It helps me handle all those ups and downs and
teaches me to trust my better instincts. It helps me to
accept what is and move on. I believed in God before
Winki died, but I took my faith for granted. Then I
almost lost that faith—my brother's death tested it to
the limit. But ultimately it grew stronger because of
what I had to go through, and that was a gift. Belief in
something bigger allows me to follow my inner com-
pass and know when to let things go. Life is too short
and too precious to get mired in the stuff I can't con-

trol. My belief in God helps me to prioritize. Going through the loss of my brother and coming out on the other side with an even closer connection to God gave me a real sense of perspective. I don't sweat the small stuff. As for the big stuff, well, I guess can handle it.

Whatever your religion or belief system, the key is to have an active inner life that radiates through all your actions in the world. We're all being tested, every day. It's not so much how bad a time we have as how *well* we handle it. That's what gives us real power. That's what God is looking at. You have to hold your head up and look at the horizon, because if you don't, if you keep gazing down at the ground, your crown's gonna fall right off.

CHAPTER 7

Strength

*People gonna let you down / Don't expect for them
to be around / They're just people . . .*
—LATIFAH, "PEOPLE"

I'd had enough. My pager was blowing up, I was
supposed to be in a million different places, and
everyone was looking for me. So I disappeared. Just
vanished. No one was gonna find me until I was good
and ready, if ever. I was done!

It was at the beginning of my career, and I was so
overscheduled that I didn't even have time to breathe.
Our company was growing. We were starting to
manage a bunch of new artists. I'd just released a new
album, and I was expected to visit at least twenty different radio stations. I had video shoots, photo shoots,
performances, store signings, interviews with this
magazine and that magazine. It's what you're supposed to do to make your career happen in this business, and I was pushing myself as hard as I could. But

I was exhausted. I tried to express myself about certain things. I tried to say it was too much, but that little people pleaser in me kept caving in. I'd say no to doing this or doing that, but apparently I wasn't forceful enough, because somehow it would end up on my schedule. And once it was on my schedule, I had to show up, because if I didn't, it would mess up my relationship with this club or that magazine or this radio station. I felt out of control, to the point where I didn't have any energy left to give. The expectations of me were so high, and I hated letting people down. But I just couldn't take it anymore.

I was doing something in the studio, putting out my tenth fire of the day, when something in me snapped. I decided to run away. I got in my car and just drove. Somehow I ended up at my brother's graveside. I bought myself a couple of Heinekens, cracked one open, and sat there drinking. I was just chillin' and having a couple of beers with my brother. Here's to you, Winki!

There I sat, on the grass beside his marker, for hours and hours. I completely lost track of time. I didn't care what I had to do or where I had to be going. I thought, "Y'all don't get it; well, you're gonna get it now!" And I got real comfortable sitting there on that grassy patch. I had to be in a dozen different places, but I stayed right where I was, far away from all the noise. The sun was shining, like it almost always was whenever I went to spend time with Winki. I just watched the geese eat the grass, glad to be someplace where no one could find me.

Do You Hear Me Now?

As the sun was setting, I went back to my car, drove home, and called my mother. Her soothing voice and wise words always have a way of calming me down. There were dozens of frantic messages on my machine, with everyone from Shakim to my assistant to the executives at the label screaming, "Where are you!" The later the message on the machine, the greater the panic in the caller's voice. I was only gone for the better part of a day, but you'd have thought I'd been kidnapped. I finally called Shakim, and when he answered he was nearly hysterical.

"Where the hell have you been? I've been looking all over for you!"

"I needed a break, Sha. It was too much."

"But Dana, why didn't you say something?"

"I tried telling you a few times."

"I'm sorry. We had so much going on, I guess I didn't hear you."

"Do you hear me now?"

And he did, for a while. I came back to the world and started from scratch again. Things would move along nicely. Then the madness would start again, and I would disappear again. I'd go hang out with Winki. We had a lot of those moments together, Winki and I.

In many ways, it was my own damn fault. The cycle continued because I had a hard time communicating how I really felt. I didn't want to hurt anyone's feelings, so I kept on extending myself to the breaking point. Fortunately or unfortunately, success came to me early, almost immediately in my career. People would think, "Wow, we've got one here." I was a moneymaking commodity and everyone was jumping on me to do different things, and I just couldn't carry it all. Our company kept growing, and there were so many things to take care of in running the business, so when it came to stuff I had to do for me personally, it got shoved to the bottom of the list. I fell into that pattern for years. When you are responsible for too many things—not to mention people who are on your payroll and counting on you for their livelihood—it can take away from who you are. You give away all the pieces of yourself until there's nothing left. That's why, at some point, you need to draw boundaries for yourself and make sure those lines don't get crossed.

Dare to Disappoint

Like many women, I can find it hard to say no. I'm sure you've been there. We feel guilty. We tend to get caught up in nurturing and pleasing others, and we lose ourselves in the process. And the more you roll in life, the more you are going to have people around you who want all that you can and cannot give. But you can't be all things to all people. You have to have something left for yourself. Accept that you will feel guilty when you say no, but say it anyway. You can still turn someone down in a nice way.

You'd be surprised at how easy it can be to let someone down gently. While you're all tangled up in guilt, fussing and fretting over how you're going to give someone what they want, or dreading their disappointment when you can't deliver, the other person probably isn't even giving it a second thought. Seriously! Think about how many times you finally did screw up the courage to say no. You probably didn't sleep the night before. You probably discussed it with your girlfriends and went round and round in circles in your mind. And when you finally said it, the other person's reaction was, "Okay, whateva." They shrugged it off or, if they *were* mad, they got over it a few days later. Yet you expended all that emotional energy building up to the big rejection. You put yourself through the whole array of resentment, guilt, and fear.

Saying no can often be better for that friendship. It's more honest. If you really can't take on a favor or give someone your time, you'll start resenting that person if you do it anyway. They're none the wiser because you said, "Sure, no problem," when it really was a problem. Not only do you hurt yourself by taking on that burden, you've damaged that relationship you're trying so hard to preserve. You've built up all this tension and turned yourself into a martyr, and nobody wants to hang out with a martyr.

"No" is a powerful word. As toddlers, when we're going through the terrible twos, we like to say it over and over again to assert our independence: "No, no, no, no, no, no!" We exult in that word, because we're discovering the joy and power of establishing our little identities. As we go through life, we have to keep practicing and say it like we mean it. No means no! But the older we get, the harder it is to say that word. We're conditioned to please. As girls, we learn to acquiesce. In school we're told not to question authority and to obey our parents and teachers. We don't want to say no to our friends for fear of being social outcasts. We eventually fall into the habit of saying yes in relationships, because we want to be loved. We don't want to risk upsetting, and possibly losing, the man in our lives. We don't want to upset our children or our family members, so we keep on saying yes to keep the peace. And the more we do it, the more we say yes when we really mean no, the more our boundaries are crossed. The more we lose ourselves.

I have a close female relative who had to see a therapist because she had such a hard time saying no. She's just too kind. I won't say who it is, because I don't want to give the wrong people ideas, but this woman can't seem to turn down anyone who asks her for help, whether it's another relative, her church, or whoever. And it's wearing her down. When she commits to something, she follows through, and she does it to perfection. She gets no sleep, she has no time for herself to just chill, and it's affecting her health. It appears as if people are taking advantage of her, but they're just so used to her willingness to help and oblivious to the fact that she has so many other obligations, because she doesn't say anything. In many ways, it's her own fault.

You have to be realistic. You are never going to please everybody. The word "no" requires a lot of practice. I am one of these people who can be a little too generous sometimes. But I think unless they are serious con artists, people tend to show you who they are. If you lend money to friends, you know which ones pay you back and which ones don't. If you lend to someone with a history of not paying back what they borrow, you might as well consider it a gift. You know the score. So you are either going to give a gift or you are not. And if you can't do it, let them know you can't do it. Try to remove the emotion from it. You shouldn't feel guilty about it. Why should this person who is asking for your help, time, or money be entitled to it? People are responsible for their own lives.

Someone in my position gets tapped a lot. In many ways I'm protected because I surround myself with real people. I don't feel the need to be at every opening or hang out on every red carpet from Los Angeles to New York. I have true friends who've known me forever. I've got Shakim, who guards me like a pit bull. Early on, there was a shooting in a nightclub where I was performing, and Shakim's first instinct was to throw his body over me to protect me from any stray bullets. The shooting wasn't actually aimed in my direction, thank God, but that was a powerful moment. The love and loyalty run that deep.

Most of my crew have been with me since before I got famous. We started hanging out together when I was fifteen, and they're like family to me. But there are always going to be a few people around who aren't so solid, and you have to learn to slowly distance yourself. Edit the takers from your life. You'll know who they are. There's no need to waste all your energy and bring the whole 'hood along. We get caught up in that just as rappers. One of us gains some success and we want to bring everybody on the block, but you just can't.

Just People

Over the years, I've learned to pull back from certain people. But it wasn't easy. When you're used to giving and being there for other people, they become familiar with that trait in you, and it's expected. A case in point is a particular friend who asked me if he could borrow money. I'd helped people out from our circle in the past, including him, but he wanted more than $1,000, and at the time I just didn't have it to give. It was around the time I went broke, in 2000. I really did not have the money. But I didn't go around sharing this fact with people, and when I said I couldn't do it, he didn't believe me. He just assumed. A lot of people love to count other people's money. They see you look a certain way or figure that because of what you do for a living you must have money in the bank all the time. But you should never assume. You don't know what another person's troubles are, because they aren't necessarily going to share them with you.

This guy took it like a personal rejection. I don't know what he was going through at the time, but he was mad, and he didn't speak to me for years. There was a falling-out over some other things, but it's usually money that brings these matters to a head. He said, "You won't even give me this money to help me feed my kids." But I didn't make those kids. I felt he was being irresponsible with his money, and when you bring children into the world, you can't afford to be reckless, and you can't make someone else, namely me, responsible for feeding your children. I said, "I wish I had the money to give to you, but I don't." It was perfectly true, but to this day I don't think he ever believed me.

And I don't feel bad about it. I can't. Even if I had that money to give, I don't think it would have been a good thing for this guy. Sometimes you enable people when you give to them. I have a cousin who is on drugs. A lot of people face this in their families, whether they choose to admit it or not. It's either drugs, or it's alcohol, or both. When they ask you for money, it's almost easier to give it to them. In your mind, you think you're actually helping this person out. But deep down in your heart, you know that $20 is going toward buying drugs, and what you are actually doing is hurting that person. They need to hit rock bottom so they can stand back up on their own. But if you're floating them, you're not helping them get to that point. They're just cruising along on your dime. If anything, you're helping to prolong the problem. You need to give them some tough love. It's the same for anyone in your life who's using your money to avoid facing their own responsibilities, even if it's just a taker friend who expects other people to help sponsor his lifestyle. If you keep subsidizing them, they'll never grow up.

My friend went on to do very well for himself, and I'm happy for him. We never talk about what happened, but we're fine now. There are always going to be different kinds of friends in your life. You have your intimate friends, your work friends, the people you know you're going to party and laugh with but you don't completely trust, and that's okay. But you have to guard your heart. You have to know who to keep at arm's length and when to protect yourself, even if that means losing a friend or two. If all they want is what they can get out of you, maybe they weren't such good friends after all.

This is just as true with female friends as it is with male friends. Not everyone's a sista. Women excel at tearing each other down. Men aren't nearly as complicated. If they like you, they'll hang out with you, and if they don't, they won't. But girls can be so competitive with each other. It stems from basic insecurity. If two attractive women can come together as friends without an agenda, it's because they already have high self-esteem. They'll party and flirt with men together and go home at the end of the night as buddies. But lots of friendships aren't as supportive and easygoing as you might think. There are girls who have to have that fat funny friend who entertains them and makes them look good when they're out together. They don't want the competition of someone who is much prettier than they are. Or they have the sidekick who's less successful or smart. Or they use you to cry about a bad relationship, then dump you the minute things get better with their man. Girlfriends have all these subtle little ways of using each other to prop themselves up. That's okay up to a point, but you have to know when to walk away.

People Are Gonna Let You Down

That's harder to do when you're younger and the line between social acceptance and self-acceptance gets blurred. My mom has seen so many examples of girls who get talked into some incredibly destructive behavior by their peer groups. Whatever one girl is into, she'll talk her friends into doing the same because she doesn't want to go it alone. The more people she drags along on her hellride, the better she feels about herself and what she's doing. There's the usual stuff, like doing drugs, getting drunk, and having sex before you're ready. Somehow girls have decided among themselves that sex is the new goodnight kiss. But there are *other* disturbing trends going on around the country—junior high and high school girls recruiting each other to perform sex acts for money or drugs. I mean, *fourteen-year-old* girls are pretending to be friends with other girls and trading them off to their dealers like pieces of junk. In return, these pimps or dealers give them dope or money for sex. And this is all happening in middle-class neighborhoods, among girls from good homes with nice families. Ladies, please! What's happening in a girl's life that could lead her down this path?

I know it's hard to let go of friendships. When you're out with your crew, that's your world. It doesn't seem like anything else is out there. But you have to shed those toxic friends for the sake of your soul. The older you get, the more you'll realize that friends come and go. The true ones who really have your back will stick around for life, and that's all you need.

I used to be more tolerant of the friends who

aren't really friends, but now I don't have time for it. I prefer the company of those who keep it real. I know what signs to look for: "Money problems and mood swings / Situations where certain people will do things." We don't need that. Life is complicated enough without the treachery of fake friends. Sure, we need people in our lives, and we need to keep our hearts open. But there has to be give and take, loyalty and sincerity, love and support. They have to pass a few litmus tests.

I've seen enough takers to spot them a mile off. There was someone in my circle who had a history of borrowing money off his friends, including me, and he was perfectly comfortable with not paying it back. I could never do that. The thought of owing somebody something would weird me out. I could never talk to that person without thinking, "Oh, he's thinking about the money I owe him and he wants it back." But some people are okay with being takers. This guy borrowed several thousand dollars from a girlfriend of mine. Meanwhile, I helped him get a job, and he started making lots of money. She'd see him around town, driving a fancy new car, owing all these people money, including her. Of course he never paid her back.

I don't mind helping people out or treating them when we're all out having a good ol' time. If I want to bring a bunch of friends along, and not everyone can afford it, it benefits me to pay for everyone, because I'm also having fun and enjoying the company. That's fair enough. My level of fun isn't always in everyone's budget. But after a while, you do start to notice the people who never reach for their wallets. You buy bottles of tequila for everyone, and there are certain people who are always the ones drinking the most, but they don't even offer to stand you one drink. These are moochers, and you should be wary of them. It's like in that episode of *Curb Your Enthusiasm* where Christian Slater is at a party eating all the caviar. Larry David tells him he has no caviar etiquette. He's just tearing into this dish like it's his own private stash, and it's probably worth hundreds of dollars. You just don't do that!

You Live and You Learn

The takers come in all forms, and it's not just about money. If you let them, people will take advantage of your time, your connections, your love, your body, and your soul. I wrote a song about this on my album *Persona*, called "People." It talks about the pitfalls of fame and the people who want to use you to get ahead: "Some they got they hands out even after you feed 'em / But they never around when you need 'em." But they're still just people. There's good and bad in all of us. It's up to you to expect nothing from others. Be aware of their motives, and move past it when they disappoint. It's also up to you to keep your radar up and be strong.

You almost have to step outside yourself and look at you as if you were someone else you really care about and really want to protect. Would you let someone take advantage of that person? Would you let someone use that person you really care about? Or would you speak up for them? If it was someone else you care about, you'd say something. I know you would. Okay, now put yourself back in that body. That person is you. Stand up and tell 'em, "Enough!"

Of course, I have to learn to take my own advice. It's hard enough for women in general to set boundaries. We're trained to give. We watch our mothers putting everyone first and themselves last. No wonder we have a tough time with the "no" word. Then there are the girls who've been sexually abused or molested. This problem is chronic. One out of four girls in America. That's a stunning statistic. Imagine, you pass by four girls walking down the street, laughing and giggling in their jeans and sneakers, and one of them has been inappropriately touched and emotionally scarred by some man—a stranger, a friend of the family, a relative, her father. She can't say no. She doesn't have a choice. Or maybe she's been told she doesn't have a choice, because this is a person in a position of authority. He tells her she'll be in trouble, or no one will believe her if she says anything. I have a friend who was molested by a relative for years. She tried telling people, but no one did believe her. People see what they want to see. Too much knowledge makes them uncomfortable. We don't create an environment where these girls feel safe about coming forward to a teacher or a parent or the police. They're ashamed and afraid they'll get shot down, so they suffer in silence for years.

I was one of those girls. When I was five years old, I was molested by the fifteen-year-old boy who was babysitting me at the time. He was not my regular babysitter. He was a shy kid from the neighborhood my dad trusted and sort of took under his wing. It went on for about a week, maybe two. But that was more than long enough to scar me for the rest of my life. That episode, and another incident a couple of years later, when I was out playing and a pervert touched me inappropriately, did some damage. I kept it locked up inside me for the next twenty years. After my brother died, I just couldn't carry it all, so I finally told my parents. My mother was devastated. She was a country girl, so at the time it happened she just wasn't up to how slick people could be. When I told my dad, he said nothing. He didn't respond. He was so furious at the person who would do that to his baby girl, his face went stone cold. It rocked his world that this was someone he put faith in. He was a cop, and very much a man of action, so I wasn't sure what he was going to do about it. It was scary.

I don't know why I didn't tell them at the time it happened. They were always very open with me. They made it easy for me to come to them about a lot of things, and no subjects were off-limits. They always did their best to be honest with me. But I just buried it as deeply as I could. There are a bunch of feelings that come with something like that: confusion, guilt, shame, grief, fear. You think somehow it was your fault. It really messes you up.

A few years ago, I finally started talking to a therapist about it. Black people tend to shy away from therapy. They believe you just suck it up and deal with it. But sometimes you need to talk to someone who'll listen and care, with no agenda. I first started seeing someone to help process the grief over my brother's death. I was having trouble tapping into some feelings for a really tough role in a movie, so my friend Jada Pinkett Smith recommended someone, and this woman really helped me. Now I have a guy who's guided me through a lot of difficult periods of my life. He's the one who finally helped me get a handle on the abuse, how it's affected me, and how I have to forgive myself.

He said: "Imagine yourself as an adult and think about what an adult can do to you. Can they beat you? Can they defeat you? No. Now, imagine yourself as that child." That really helped me get a perspective on what happened to me. I was just a baby. I had no power or control over the situation. I wish I'd said something sooner, because I always wondered, "Did he do that to someone else?" But at the time it happened, it was all way beyond my comprehension. When I was old enough to understand, the time for action had passed.

I stopped blaming myself, because I realized that I was totally being taken advantage of. My guilt came from the fact that I didn't scream or run right back to my parents and tell them. They explained my body parts to me, they told me not to talk to strangers. They communicated to me as much as they possibly could. But I still had the mind of a child. And this was a babysitter, not a stranger. He was someone with authority over me, someone who had been entrusted with my care. To a five-year-old, that's a confusing situation. You think you are smart enough and you are doing the right thing, but you are being taken advantage of by someone bigger, stronger, and depraved enough to manipulate and violate a child.

I don't know how this affects other women. I can't speak for everyone. But I would imagine, if there's a repeat pattern of abuse, a lot of girls end up gravitating toward abusive relationships, because it's what they know. They get locked in a cycle of victimhood, and their boundaries get broken over and over again.

Fight Back

In my case, it was the opposite. The older I got, and the more I was able to protect myself, the more I *did* protect myself. When I was about ten years old and we first moved into our house on Littleton Avenue from the projects, my mother sent me to the corner to buy some milk, and on my way home some man on the street tried to grab my behind. Now, I was big for my age, and I started developing early, but I was still clearly a child. And I was heated. I'd been violated once before, and no way, nohow, was it gonna happen again. I mustered all the strength I could and slapped him in the face so hard, I left a nice red mark on his cheek. He swung right back at me, and I went running home with a black eye, but I was proud of myself. I fought back.

When my mom saw my face, she was horrified,

but then I told her what happened. She was proud of the way I fought back. The fact that her little girl had the courage to stand up when lines were crossed gave her comfort. She told a neighbor, whose son was known and respected among the different crews in the area, and he went with me and my mother around the streets of our community, stepping on corners and knocking on doors to tell certain people, "You see this girl? She's off-limits! Don't touch, or you answer to me!"

By the time I hit my teens, I was very aware of personal boundaries. I went through a promiscuous phase. I was sexually curious at an early age, which tends to happen when you get introduced to things you shouldn't even know about when you're a child. But when I did experiment, I was in control, or at least I thought I was. Emotionally, I kept everyone at a distance.

That hurt me in my dating life. I had boyfriends, but between the sexual abuse and my parents separating and eventually divorcing, I didn't have much faith in relationships. I definitely didn't trust guys. Sure, there were great men in my life, like my father and my brother and a lot of platonic male friends and even a few boyfriends; but after what happened to me, I was convinced that romantically, things just weren't meant to work out. I had a certain confusion in my relationships and major commitment issues. I could have been married a long time ago had I not been so self-protective. In my personal life, I didn't just have boundaries, I had ten-foot walls!

I'm getting better at it, but dating has always been my Achilles' heel. I was able to excel at other stuff much more easily. I had a clearer understanding of what to do in order to make things happen. But when it came to my personal life, in my mind I made it much more complicated than it needed to be. And it didn't help that I would watch men with a certain eye, especially when they were around kids. I know plenty of guys who are great with kids, and wonderful parents, but I still take an extra look at people. If I see a little girl on a man's lap, and I think she's been there a little too long, I get suspicious, especially if he's not the father. I just don't trust it. I've been through it, and I know how subtle and sneaky sexual deviance can be. These guys always have this in the backs of their minds, and they're always looking for opportunities to act out those ideas on some kid. Most people don't think that way, but once you know, you know, and in a lot of ways I wish I didn't have that knowledge.

As a result of all that happened to me early in life, my personal boundaries are a little too strong at times, yet I allow my business boundaries to get

broken all the time. (I tend to go in extremes.) I'm
better about saying no, but it's a constant balancing
act, and when things get out of whack, it can really
mess me up.

About six years ago, after *Chicago*, my career was
going gangbusters, and Shakim and I were saying yes
to just about every opportunity that came our way. I
worked three times harder than I ever had in my life,
and I'd always worked pretty hard to begin with. I
was doing two or three movies a year, plus my music
career, and multiple endorsement deals, including
my CoverGirl partnership. For three years, I did not
take a vacation. The most I could get was a Sunday
off, but even then my phone was always ringing. It
got to the point where I was constantly exhausted.
But I still had to get up, put on a happy face, do the
interviews, make the appearances, turn up at the
award shows. I had all these things to do, and there
was no way I could get out of doing them if I really
wanted to make these different branches of my career
a success. If you want certain things in life, you have
to show up, no matter how you are feeling that day.

To deal with the fact that I wasn't going to be able
to take a break in the middle of all this, I started to
drink. I began to have a few drinks at night just to
unwind. But the amount I was drinking increased
over time. This can happen to a lot of people who do

what I do. When you're on a set fourteen hours a day for three to six months straight, there's no time to unwind. You come home late at night, then go back out to the set early the next morning. In between, alcohol becomes a way to unwind. Add to that the fact that acting wasn't my only job. On weekends, I had my business to run and a music career to maintain. It didn't stop. Because I was working so hard, I felt entitled to party hard. But it was getting out of control, and I was losing Dana Owens under all of that.

Finally, Shakim said something: "Dana, are you okay?" He'd noticed my drinking, and he was getting worried. "You know there's nothing I wouldn't do for you. I just want to make sure you're all right."

"You know what, Sha, I don't think I am okay. As a matter of fact, I think I may be drowning over here."

That conversation gave us the opportunity to check in with each other. We had a real heart-to-heart, and I expressed everything I was feeling about my life and how I felt that it wasn't even my life anymore, because I was living on everyone else's schedule. He shared a few of the things that he was going through, and we came together as friends. We decided we would make some changes. One major change was that I was going to start taking vacations. I was going to do what the Italians do and take off the entire month of August. They've got it right. They take breaks in the middle of the day, eat good food, and enjoy a nice glass of wine. They take time off to decompress and enjoy life.

Mental Health Break

But I didn't take just the month-long vacations. I also stopped working on Sundays. Even God rested on the seventh day, and if He needs a break, so do I. Even if it's just for a few hours on that one day, to relax in your own space, do it! I found a way to incorporate little escapes into my schedule year-round, even if it just means a drive to some country inn an hour away. And I have one hard-and-fast rule that I stick to: "I am out of town and unavailable. *Don't call me!*"

There are lots of different ways to take a vacation, even if you can't afford a month off to travel somewhere exotic. Some people just need that time first thing in the morning to go to the gym, where they can't take any calls and there's no one to bother them. For some women, it's going to the spa and having a massage. Some people wake up and meditate or read their holy book, whatever that may be. It's their time with themselves, and it should be sacrosanct.

For me, it's taking a few minutes out of my day to just breathe. Yoga taught me how to concentrate on the breath, and it's been a helpful tool for finding balance in my life. Before I go to bed at night, especially if I can't sleep, I just sit and take ten deep breaths. When I get up in the morning, I give myself ten minutes to clear my head of all the clutter. I just clear my mind or think of something positive. I switch off my phone and concentrate on breathing and stretching, trying not to focus on anything else that's coming my way. And somehow it works. When I start my day like that, I feel so much more positive and prepared for whatever it is I have to face. Like the August vacation, when I come back all recharged and ready to conquer the world, this mini mental break helps me decompress and frees my spirit.

Just breathe. Take ten minutes. Even if you just have to lock yourself in the bathroom. Take that time to be with yourself, by yourself.

Yoga's a great way to get back in touch with yourself. It teaches you to move and stretch toward your pain. When you're holding certain poses, that pain becomes a measure of where you are, physically and emotionally, and the more you do it, the farther you can get. The pain makes you aware of the moment. I'm no yogi or guru, but I've learned over the years that sometimes we run away from the pain, and when we do that, when we mask the pain, our emotional issues tend to pile up like a bunch of dirty laundry. You can't think straight in a space that's all cluttered like that. But when you run toward the pain and face it down, you can get rid of it.

It all comes back to boundaries. Whether it's your personal life, your business dealings, or even just your relationship with yourself, your soul needs to strike that balance between yes and no. I'm not perfect. I get thrown off balance very easily. This past year has been hectic, and I haven't taken the time for myself I needed. There was too much to get done. That's why I am glad I'm writing this book. I'm going to go back and read my own words, again and again. It will be a reminder to me to heed my own advice. So, Dana, if you're reading this for the tenth, twentieth, or hundredth time, here it is:

Take the time to check in with yourself, regularly. Don't lose yourself. Love yourself.

CHAPTER 8

Joy

The more you praise and celebrate your life,
the more there is in life to celebrate.
—OPRAH WINFREY

I put my hands over my eyes before they lifted up the cover, for maximum impact. Then I saw it. That beautiful new star on the Hollywood Walk of Fame. I reached out to touch it—to make sure it was real. Then I ran my hands over my name in polished brass. I caressed the shiny pink granite embedded in the ground. This was it. I made it. And it was all the more special because I was with the people who believed in me the whole time. That morning of January 6, 2006, was a moment of pure, unadulterated joy that I will never forget. It had to be, hands down, one of the best moments of my life. Dad was to my right and Mom was to my left, and friends and family were all around me. The look was all over my face. I was like a little kid kneeling on the red carpet, squealing with delight. My heart was also overflowing with love and appreciation for my fans. They lifted me up and got me to that point. Without them, none of this would have been possible. I wanted to tell each and every one of them how much their support meant to me. I said:

"Stay up, peace, and I love you, fans, fans, fans! It's you who made queen, *Queen!*"

Mom, who presented the star to me, gave a speech that summed it up perfectly:

"Who would have known that in the seventies, when a pink eight-pound baby girl was born, this is where she would be today? She came out screaming, 'Look out, world, here I come!'"

Who would have known?

Savor It

We have to savor these moments for all they're worth. They're not permanent. They don't happen every day, and they may never happen again. I got real comfortable down there on that sidewalk. I blew my star a kiss. I didn't want to leave!

I didn't even know until that day that I was the first hip-hop artist to ever get a star on the Walk of Fame. It's one of the few forms of recognition I really wanted. That star is inspiration. It's someone's dream. I remember walking down Hollywood Boulevard when I was seventeen and seeing all those names and thinking, "Wow, look at that! That's so-and-so and so-and-so. I would love to be able to do that." I knew the only way of being able to get that kind of recognition was to accomplish a lot. So for me to have come from where I'm from, a regular girl from Newark, New Jersey, it was confirmation that, yes, you *can* do anything.

I felt like my life had come full circle. Some other girl from the 'hood is going to walk the Walk of Fame, look down and see my name, and think, "Wow, she's from Newark like me!" Or, "Wow, she's a bigger girl like me!" "If she can do it, I can do it!"

And it can't get more real than the ground under your feet. They gave me a prime piece of real estate, right next to Michael Jackson's tile near the northwest corner of Hollywood and North Orange. I have a music legend right next door to me. It doesn't matter how many people walk on top of it. The star doesn't have to be spit-shined. It's right there, in a location where everybody can see it. It'll be there after I'm gone. My place. We all want a place. We all want to feel as if we contributed. We all want to be acknowledged. That doesn't happen by having everything handed to you. It happens only when you strive for it. That star was proof that, yeah, I've done a couple of things.

We kept the celebrations going all day. I did some interviews, then we all had lunch and hung out for a few hours. Then some friends threw me a party at the Standard Hotel. We had a blast. The music was great, and all of us—my mom, my dad, my entire extended family, all of my closest friends, and I—danced the night away.

You've got to celebrate. Like I learned when Winki died, life isn't promised, and those special moments need to be cherished for whatever they are, whether they're a graduation, a promotion, a wedding day, or even a small thing like losing five pounds. We get so caught up in our business that too often we forget how to live, and we miss all those moments that should be giving us joy.

There's no point in taking a big bite out of life unless you take the time to savor the flavor. Some women never learn how to do this enough. They let the belief that they aren't good enough hold them back. They downplay their successes, almost apologizing for them. We're quick to recognize and support others in their achievements, but we put the words "I'm just" in front of our job title or role in life, as if it's not even worthy of a mention. We need to do better for ourselves. The queen inside us demands it. Whether it's a promotion or something as small as learning a new computer skill or getting through a checklist of errands, we have to learn to say to ourselves, "Good job! I'm proud of you!"

You don't have to tell me to celebrate. I'm the girl who's quick to throw a party. But it wasn't always that way. When I won my first Grammy, I barely felt it. I was so deep in my grief over Winki's death that the moment came and went. But I've made up for it since then. When I found out I was nominated for a best supporting actress Oscar for *Chicago*, I was like a little kid on Christmas morning. I'd just come home from spending the weekend in Atlanta. I'd been up all night on the tour bus, watching the first season of *Good Times* in its entirety. It was drafty on the bus and I couldn't sleep. When I finally got home I headed straight to bed, and I'd just slipped under the covers, all comfy cozy, when Shakim called me. He said:

"Yo, we got the nomination!"

"What nomination?"

"The Oscar nomination."

"No waaaaaay!"

I went jumping, running, and screaming around the house. I called all my friends and woke them up. My assistant was downstairs sleeping, so I dived on top of her and woke her up. I said, "Yo, we got it!"

It was a special moment, because it was so un-expected.

No Moment Too Small

Oscar nominations, Grammy wins, a star on Hollywood Boulevard—these are all big deals. But they're not the only moments I celebrate. I take the time to appreciate even the simplest things in life. I want every day to be life for the living, not just traipsing through it and existing. I want to be in the present.

Too often, I see people plugged into their Black-Berrys, iPhones, or computers. Either they need constant distractions or they feel like they have to capture every moment on their camera phones and blog their thoughts to the entire world. Somehow that's more important to them than having a face-to-face conversation with someone who's actually in the same room. That's no way to live. You're missing out on so much. Some of my most treasured memories are those times my brother and I sat around the family dinner table with our parents, just talking to each other. Those are the special moments, if for no other reason than that it's where you want to be and everything in your world is right. No fanfare. No golden statues. Just chillin' and passing the time with the people you love.

After dinner, Mom and Dad would have us read sections of the newspaper out loud, so they could see how we were doing in our reading and comprehension. If we didn't understand a word, they'd make us go look it up in a dictionary and they'd teach us how to pronounce it. We'd surprise them later on by using it correctly in a sentence. Those conversations made us want to read more and learn. They were invaluable lessons. You can't do that when your kids are texting each other and you're checking your crackberry every five seconds for messages. Have you seen all those people walking around outside, talking on their cell phones? It could be the most perfect day of the summer, but they're blind to it. Their bodies are there, but their minds are somewhere else.

No moment is too inconsequential to explore. It could be something as small as feeling the cool breeze on my face, enjoying a walk by the beach with a good friend, or just kicking back at my mother's house, drinking iced tea and watching all the wildlife in the woods at the edge of her backyard in New Jersey. She's feeding a whole family of raccoons back there!

My favorite vacation of all time was a trip I took with my mother to Cabo San Lucas, Mexico, a few years ago. It was special because it was just the two of us—a mother-and-daughter trip. Nothing was planned. We just did things on the spur of the moment. One day I convinced her to ride a wave runner with me. Another time we took a golf lesson together, and I saw that Mom had quite the swing, like me! I thought, "Oh, so that's where I get it from."

We decided to rent a Jeep and take a drive to the original Hotel California in Todos Santos, an artists' colony about a forty-five-minute drive away. We ate lunch at the hotel, explored the streets, and talked to some of the artists in their galleries. Finding that place on our own, we felt like a couple of intrepid explorers.

Back in Cabo, Mom bonded with a woman at the hotel who was on the food services staff. She recommended a restaurant in town where her husband worked, so that night we tried it. The food was great, but we got torn up by mosquitoes. It was so bad that we had to leave before dinner was over. It was painful. We were scratching ourselves and slapping each other's arms and legs every time one of those little beasts landed on us. But we were laughing so hard! It was just one of those funny moments that we got to experience together.

We shared a two-bedroom suite, and one night we decided to go to bed early. Mom went to her room, and I went to my room and flicked on the television. All of a sudden, I could hear laughter coming from the other side of the suite. And every time I heard the laughter, I was laughing myself. We were both watching something and laughing in the same spots. I went into my mother's room and asked her, "What are you watching?" It was *Napoleon Dynamite*. Of all the English satellite channels to choose from, we'd both stumbled on that movie. Neither of us had seen it before, so we decided to watch it together. We were on the floor, howling with laughter. It doesn't get any better than that.

When I look at the pictures from that vacation, I look so happy just to be hanging out with my best friend in the world. What made it memorable was the spontaneity of it. We were completely in the moment. I promised myself we'd do it every year, and for the most part, we have. Together, we're gonna cover the globe.

Go for Broke

I have great moments on the road with my dad, too. When we're traveling, he drives for me and runs my security. He's a former special ops guy, and he spent years as an undercover cop, so the man has eyes in the back of his head. But he also knows how to roll. He understands how to adapt to any situation and get the most out of it. We had a ball when we were filming

Last Holiday. We hung out in New Orleans, Austria, Czechoslovakia. We explored the bohemian world of Prague, where all the backpackers and intellectuals like to hang. But mostly we gambled! Dad comes from a long line of professional gamblers. He's not compulsive about it. He's just so damn good at it. He taught me how to shoot pool, bet on horses, play craps, poker, the roulette wheel. Man, he cleaned up at the casinos in Europe. He won more than 30,000 euros one night. Dad was gambling with Timothy Hutton, and he taught Tim his method. They'd play a little blackjack, progress to a certain point, then go back to the roulette table. He explained the denominations of the chips, which are square in European casinos, not round, and he warned Tim to make sure he cashed those chips when they got to a certain amount, so he could appreciate their full value—the euro value of what he was actually gambling with— and walk away ahead of the game. "Don't treat those chips like confetti," he said. Tim made some serious winnings that night, too.

Good gamblers really know how to live in the moment. Scared money never wins. You also have to know that once you hit it big in a game, the odds of it happening again are slim and you should walk away. But you have to play the game to play the game. It's for the amusement of it. Once you start telling yourself, "I gotta win this, I can't afford to lose that," you're sunk. It's just like life itself. Play to win!

My dad and I have a ball wherever we go. Doing thirty cities on a tour bus can get pretty monotonous, so we laugh and joke and tell stories. I love the simple stuff, like pulling into a Waffle House for breakfast or doing a little shopping at Wal-Mart. People do a double take when they see Queen Latifah in these places, but they're always respectful and friendly. They usually want to chat and take a picture or get an autograph, and I've had some pleasant conversations with regular people when I've been out on the road. A couple of years ago, we even stopped at Six Flags Magic Mountain to go on a few rides. It was hot that day, and we started running around and squirting water at each other from our plastic squeeze bottles. People couldn't believe what they were seeing—a celebrity doing the same things they like to do, having fun with friends and family.

My dad learned how to live every day like it was his last when he was fighting in Vietnam. He knew he was lucky if he survived yesterday. He knew that when he said good-bye to a friend, it might be the last time he ever saw him. Maybe the circumstances forced things to an extreme level, but he made every moment as rip-roaring as he could. He went hell for broke.

No Regrets

After I made *Last Holiday*, a journalist asked me what I would do if someone told me I had only three weeks to live. My answer would still be the same. I'd go hell for broke, too. I'd definitely spend time with my family and friends. Then I'd probably go somewhere I really wanted to go, like a safari in Africa or the Great Wall of China. Or I'd just hang out in Jamaica and drink a Red Stripe and relax. Just enjoy the water. I would enjoy nature. I'd look at the sky, swim, and hold babies. Since I wouldn't have time to have one, I'd hold my little nephew. And watch the kids laugh, 'cause they always crack me up when they laugh. They'll laugh at anything. I'd seek out the simple pleasures, then get ready to get on up out of here.

And I'd have no regrets. I would not change a thing.

If I ran into a nineteen-year-old version of myself, I'd just tell her to live, full out. I might also tell her to go ahead and have a few babies and not worry about the timing of it. But mostly I'd tell her that she's stronger than she thinks, and she shouldn't doubt herself on her path. I'd say:

"Dana. Do you know who you *are*? Guess who you get to be! And guess what, you even get to lose weight! No, you good, you good. You just keep doing your thing!"

And I'd say the same thing to you:

Celebrate. Make every moment count. Walk tall. Wear your crown with pride.